100 WALKS IN
CHESHIRE

THE CROWOOD PRESS

First published in 2016 by
The Crowood Press Ltd
Ramsbury, Marlborough
Wiltshire SN8 2HR

www.crowood.com

British Library Cataloguing-in-Publication Data
A catalogue record for this book is available from the British Library.

ISBN 978 1 78500 181 9

Front cover: Shutterstock

Mapping in this book is sourced from the following products: OS Explorer 257; 266; 267;
268; 276

© Crown copyright 2016 Ordnance Survey. Licence number 100038003

Every effort has been made to ensure the accuracy of this book. However, changes can
occur during the lifetime of an edition. The Publishers cannot be held responsible for any
errors or omissions or for the consequences of any reliance on the information given in
this book, but should be very grateful if walkers could let us know of any inaccuracies by
writing to us at the address above or via the website.

As with any outdoor activity, accidents and injury can occur. We strongly advise readers to
check the local weather forecast before setting out and to take an OS map. The Publishers
accept no responsibility for any injuries which may occur in relation to following the walk
descriptions contained within this book.

Graphic design and layout by Peggy Issenman, www.peggyandco.ca
Printed and bound in India by Replika Press Pvt. Ltd.

Contents

How to Use this Book

The walks in the book are ordered by distance, starting with the shortest. An information panel for each walk shows the distance, start point (see below), a summary of route terrain and level of difficulty (Easy/Moderate/Difficult), OS map(s) required, and suggested pubs/cafés at the start/end of walk or en route.

MAPS

There are 89 maps covering the 100 walks. Some of the walks are extensions of existing routes and the information panel for these walks will tell you the distance of the short and long versions of the walk.

The routes marked on the maps are punctuated by a series of numbered waypoints. These relate to the same numbers shown in the walk description.

Start Points

The start of each walk is given as a postcode and also a six-figure grid reference number prefixed by two letters (which indicates the relevant square on the National Grid). More information on grid references is found on Ordnance Survey maps.

Parking

Many of the car parks suggested are public, but for some walks you will have to park on the roadside or in a lay-by. Please be considerate when leaving your car and do not block access roads or gates. Also, if parking in a pub car park for the duration of the walk, please try to avoid busy times.

COUNTRYSIDE CODE
- Consider the local community and other people enjoying the outdoors
- Leave gates and property as you find them and follow paths
- Leave no trace of your visit and take litter home
- Keep dogs under effective control
- Plan ahead and be prepared
- Follow advice and local signs

Walks Locator

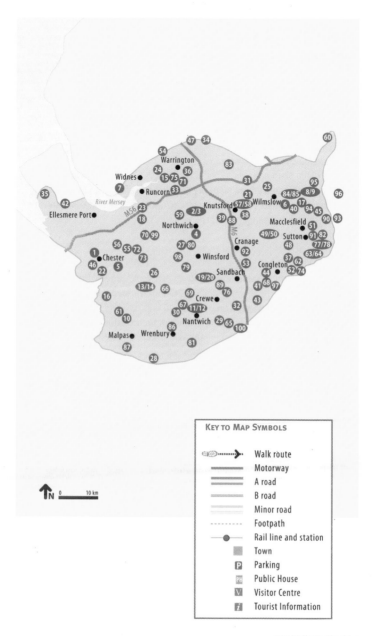

KEY TO MAP SYMBOLS

- Walk route
- Motorway
- A road
- B road
- Minor road
- Footpath
- Rail line and station
- Town
- **P** Parking
- **PH** Public House
- **V** Visitor Centre
- **i** Tourist Information

Chester City Walls

START King Charles Tower, Chester, CH1 3EH, GR SJ406 667

DISTANCE 2½ miles (4km)

MAPS OS Landranger 117 Chester & Wrexham; OS Explorer 266 Wirral & Chester

WHERE TO EAT AND DRINK There are many outlets to suit all tastes in Chester

A walk around one of England's most complete walled towns.

The walk around the old town walls of Chester is one of the highlights not only of a visit to the city itself, but also of a visit to Cheshire. The route directions are minimal as the walk merely follows the wall top, but are given for completeness.

⬚1 King Charles Tower stands close to the Shropshire Union Canal, which threads its way through the city. Go up the steps onto the wall and turn right. On this first section of wall you will pass the city's Cathedral to the right. Continue to Eastgate, the most picturesque of the gates that pierce the walls. Next, the walk takes you over Newgate.

⬚2 To the left here is the Roman amphitheatre. Continue to the corner overlooking the River Dee. Turn right, with the wall, to reach Bridgegate.

⬚3 At the next corner, the Castle is to the right, while to the left is the Roodee, Chester racecourse.

⬚4 Now walk to Watergate and continue to the final corner and the linked Bonewoldsthorne and Water Towers. Turn right and cross St Martin's Gate and Northgate to return to the start point.

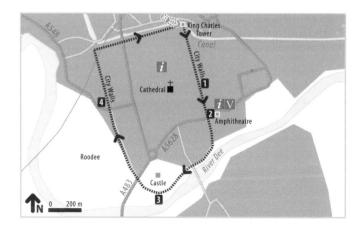

Points of interest

 King Charles Tower: the name derives from an old legend that King Charles stood here on 24 September 1645 and watched his army being defeated at the battle of Rowton Moor.

Chester Cathedral: This is the old abbey church for a Benedictine monastery founded in 1092 by Hugh Lupes, the Norman Earl of Chester. Only after the Dissolution did it become the city's cathedral. Inside there is some superbly carved woodwork, particularly on the fourteenth-century choir stalls.

Roman amphitheatre: During the first century AD the Romans occupied the site on the banks of the River Dee known as *Deva*. Soon it became an important military base, the headquarters for one of three British legions. The Romans fortified *Deva*, and two sections of that wall can still be seen between Northgate and King Charles Tower. The amphitheatre is the largest so far discovered in Britain. When completed, it was of stone and measured 315 by 285ft. The gladiatorial area measured 190 by 160ft. The best of the excavated Roman remains are to be found in the Grosvenor Museum in Grosvenor St.

Chester Castle: The first known castle on the site was built in 1070 by William the Conqueror. This motte and bailey structure was later consolidated, the thirteenth-century stone castle being an important centre during Edward's campaigns in Wales. However, from the fifteenth century the castle fell into disrepair. Today, only the square Agricola Tower and Flag Tower remain of the medieval building, the rest having been built in the late eighteenth century.

Watergate: In medieval times, when boats were smaller and the River Dee a more navigable waterway, Chester was an important port, the Watergate giving access to the dock area, which was protected by the Water Tower. At that time it is likely that the Water Tower actually stood in water. However, changes in drainage patterns caused the Dee to silt up. Chester declined as a port and the river retreated from both Watergate and the Water Tower.

Marbury Country Park

START Marbury Country Park car park, CW9 6AT, GR SJ652 763

DISTANCE 2½ miles (4km); 4 miles (6.5km) with extension

MAPS OS Explorer 267 Northwich & Delamere Forest

WHERE TO EAT AND DRINK Stanley Arms, Anderton (close by the Anderton Boat Lift), To1606 75059

An easy walk in both instances, with the short walk going around the edges of the Park and the extension taking in the Anderton Boat Lift.

Route 2

1 Leave the car park by the north-east exit path and shortly turn left. Follow this track past the toilet and information centre until facing Budworth Mere. Go forwards until a path to the left is visible. Turn right and follow the footpath for about 250yds and take the left fork back into the Park (Marbury La). Follow this road for about 1,200yds to a canal bridge and cross over it.

2 Drop down to the canal and go east to the next bridge in about 200yds. Cross over it, then follow the path to the right for about 800yds, then take the right fork down to the edge of Budworth Mere for a further 600yds to the boathouse. In a further 200yds at the bird hides turn left and up steps.

Route 3

1 For the extension, turn right and go about 70yds before crossing the road to a concrete bus shelter. Just beyond the shelter turn left through a kissing gate into fields. Go into the left-hand field, keeping close to the hedge on the right. At the end of the field go into the woodland section and cross the footbridge and up the bank to exit in another field. Follow the path through two fields and cross Cogshall La into another field. Follow the hedge line to the right across two fields and turn left into Hough La. Go down the hill for about 550yds and across the canal bridge.

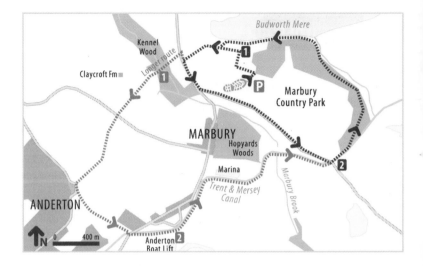

Turn left and shortly take a short path to the right down and turn right onto the canal towpath.

② Follow the towpath for 400yds to the Anderton Boat Lift. Then go along the towpath for about 1 mile to the Marbury Lane Bridge. Follow the short route from this point back to the car park.

Anderton Boat Lift: 'The Cathedral of the Canals' is a unique Victorian piece of cast iron engineering. Built in 1875, it was used to transfer barges from the Trent and Mersey Canal to the River Weaver – a drop of 50ft. It has a visitors' centre, where boat trips can be booked.

Marbury Country Park: Set by Budworth Mere, the Park offers a wide range of activities including fishing, swimming in the open air pool, exploring the garden centre and an arboretum.

Budworth Mere: Used for sailing, fishing (club only), birdwatching and openwater swimming (club only).

START The Weaver Hall Museum and Workhouse car park, CW9 8AB, GR SJ658 732

DISTANCE 2½ miles (4km)

MAPS OS Landranger 118 Stoke-on-Trent & Macclesfield; OS Explorer 267 Northwich & Delamere Forest

WHERE TO EAT AND DRINK There are numerous possibilities in Northwich

A short but fascinating town walk.

1 Leave the car park and turn left, passing under the viaduct and turning immediately left, walking beside the arches of the viaduct to the River Weaver. Turn left again and walk beside the river, continuing along until you reach the first footbridge, which is a swing bridge. Cross this and the Hunt's Locks beyond (the locks are on another arm of the River Weaver) and walk to a path junction. Continue ahead, bearing left at first and then swinging right just before steps to go under the railway viaduct again. Continue to reach a road.

2 Turn right along the road (Spencer St, which leads into Navigation Rd), as far as a T–junction. Turn right into Chester Way, go over the bridge over the River Weaver and then drop down left to follow a path beside the river at Hayhurst Quay. You soon cross another bridge; turn right, crossing over the road and following the river to reach a road. Cross straight over to rejoin the path and continue along it.

3 Soon the path is sandwiched between the railway viaduct and the river. Follow the line of the viaduct, crossing the river and continuing to reach London Rd (the main A533), and walking beneath the viaduct back to the start at the museum car park.

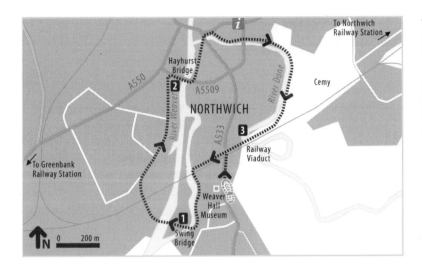

Points of interest

Railway viaduct: The superb viaduct took the Cheshire railway over the rivers and canals of Northwich. Its 48 arches are over ½ mile long and took the railway 40ft above the water. It is now a Grade II-listed structure.

Swing bridge: This elegant footbridge is also Grade II-listed. It can be swung to allow boats to traverse this older course of the River Weaver.

Bridge: This is the Hayhurst Bridge, built in 1898. It is also a swing bridge, though only tall boats would require it to do so. Hayhurst is widely believed to have been the first electrically driven swing bridge in Britain.

The Weaver Hall Museum and Workhouse: Interesting displays and tales of the history and industry of west Cheshire housed within the old Northwich Union Workhouse building.

START Christleton church,
CH3 7AP, GR SJ441 657

DISTANCE 2½ miles (4km)

MAPS OS Landranger 117
Chester & Wrexham; OS Explorer
266 Wirral & Chester

WHERE TO EAT AND DRINK
The Ring O' Bells Inn,
Christleton, T01244 335422

A walk along the Shropshire Union Canal and by an ancient battlefield.

1 From the church in Christleton, walk to the triangular village green
(an unusual feature, village greens being uncommon in Cheshire), on
which the old pump house and pump still stand, and head south past
the Ring O' Bells Inn, continuing along the road past a school to a road
junction. Walk down Rowton Bridge Rd, going over the Shropshire
Union Canal to reach the A41. Cross, with great care, and follow the road
opposite. This soon passes the site of the battle of Rowton Moor. Continue
along the road through Rowton village to reach a T–junction and turn left,
continuing until you reach the A41 again.

2 Cross over and follow the road opposite, called Moor La. This soon
goes right. Ignore all side turnings to reach a crossroads in Waverton; now
turn left. At the canal bridge turn left down onto the towpath and follow
it back to the bridge that was crossed at Rowton Bridge Rd. Turn right up
onto the road and reverse the outward route through Christleton to return
to the start.

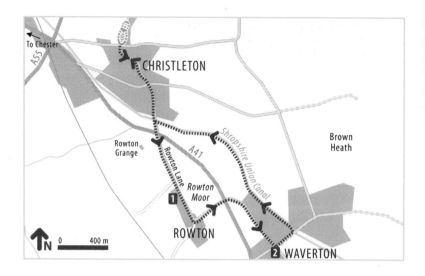

Points of interest

🔍 **Shropshire Union Canal:** The Union of the name was the amalgamation of several companies into a single company, creating a web-like system that reached as far as Llangollen and Wolverhampton, as well as linking into the Trent and Mersey on the Cheshire Ring. The network formed a powerful commercial highway, and is still one of the best canal systems in Britain.

Rowton Moor: During the Civil War, Chester was a Royalist stronghold and by late 1644 was under a state of siege. The siege was long and hard, and, in an effort to lift it and, in part, to link up with the Royalist army of the Marquis of Montrose to the north in Lancashire, the King marched north in September 1645. On 24 September, the King's cavalry met the Parliamentary army of Major General Poyntz here at Rowton Moor and was heavily defeated. The battle was one of the last set-piece actions of the first Civil War.

Christleton: This village was mentioned in the Domesday Book, and almost six centuries later the Old Hall, the oldest village house, was the headquarters of the Parliamentarians besieging Chester.

Alderley Edge & Hough

START National Trust car park
on the B5087, GR SJ859 773

DISTANCE 3 miles (5km)

MAPS OS Landranger 118 Stoke-on-
Trent & Macclesfield; OS Explorer 268
Wilmslow, Macclesfield & Congleton

WHERE TO EAT AND DRINK
The Wizard, Alderley Edge (tea room
at the back open at weekends,
children welcome, dogs allowed in
outside area only), To1625 584 000;
there are many cafés, pubs and a
supermarket in Alderley Edge

An easy walk, not strenuous, but on the Edge beware as route-finding can be
confusing and difficult.

1 From the car park head towards the information board and along to
a gate. Turn right and go down a track a short distance before turning left
in front of The Bungalow and along a well-maintained track. When you
enter a clearing ahead, passing by 'Engine Vein' mine works, go straight
across it to join a path which bears to the left. Continue ahead over cross
tracks and at the next cross track, just before a stone wall, bear right and
uphill towards the remains of the Armada Beacon.

From the Beacon turn your back to the wall and go down a short
distance to meet a track and turn to the right on a main path that will take
you to an open, rocky viewpoint at Alderley Edge. The views from here
extend from the Welsh hills to the west to the Derbyshire Peak District to
the east on a clear day. You will also find some caves here, but take care if
you do go into them, particularly if you have children with you.

With the view in front of you, turn left to walk through woods
following a yellow marker post. Following this path to a dip, you veer to
the right over a small rise before dropping steeply down the hillside. This
path emerges at a barbed wire fence and a field; turn left here and follow
the path to the road. Turn left, then right across the road to follow a public
footpath sign to Saddlebole Farm.

2 At the end of the drive go left over a stile to enter a field. Keep the
hedge on your right and pass through a metal gate, keeping right to cross
a field to another road. At the road turn right and after 550yds turn right
again down a footpath signposted 'Mottram', which lies opposite the
entrance of Brook Farm. Walk across the large field, keeping the hedge to
your left, until you reach a stile. Over the stile is a small pool on your left;

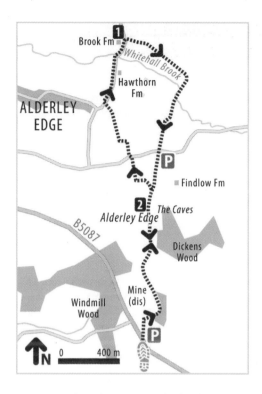

you turn to the right. Cross a stile ahead and turn right again, following a sign for 'The Edge'.

Cross a footbridge and a stile and go left diagonally, keeping the hedge on your left, to go over two more stiles, up a path (can be muddy in parts) and onto the road. Over the road is an upward path in a sunken lane, and where this enters a wood take any of the paths going up, as they should all lead back near to the open rocky outcrop. From here follow the green NT waymarkers back to the car park.

Points of interest

The Caves: These date back to the early eighteenth century, when mainly copper ore was mined here. Engine Vein (now filled in) had fine examples of copper on a fault plane, with cobalt blue azurite nodules to be found.

Alderley Edge: 600ft high, with excellent views of the Cheshire Plain. There was once a Neolithic settlement here. Bronze Age pottery and tools have been discovered in the area.

Hale Village & the Mersey Shore

START The car park in front of a row of shops in Hale, L24 4AX, GR SJ469 825

DISTANCE 3 miles (5km)

MAPS OS Landranger 108 Liverpool, Southport & Wigan; OS Explorer 275 Liverpool, St Helens, Widnes & Runcorn

WHERE TO EAT AND DRINK
The Childe of Hale, T0151 425 2954

An easy walk on good surfaced footpaths from an interesting village and beside the Mersey Estuary.

① Turn right from the car park and walk for 100yds before turning left as the road forks to a traffic island with a stone cross on it. Go down the lane for another 100yds to the Childe of Hale Inn, a favourite with walkers who enjoy a 'log fire' atmosphere.

② Beyond the Childe of Hale the road splits into two. Take the right-hand fork into Church End, past the thatched cottages. After 200yds take Church Rd and follow it to St Mary's church on your left. Pass the church and continue for a further ½ mile through a landscape of agricultural farmland.

③ On reaching a gateway pass through and take a footpath, the Mersey Way, to Hale lighthouse about 600yds away.

At the lighthouse a right of way signpost directs you to Within, which you follow for the next ¾ mile. The footpath follows the contours of the Mersey Estuary and stands high on a bank above areas of saltmarsh, rich in wildlife. At the gate turn left and walk inland back onto Within Way and follow the lane for the next mile back into the village of Hale. It emerges in Church Rd, opposite the large Manor House where the poet John Betjeman stayed and wrote 'The Manor House, Hale'. Turning right into Church Rd, retrace your steps for a short while back to the start.

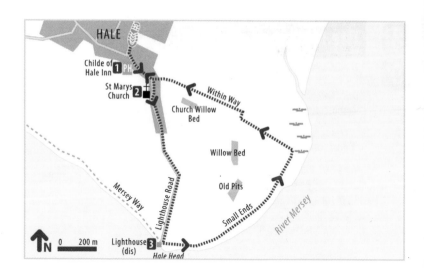

Points of interest

St Mary's church: This ancient church is famed as the last resting place of John Middleton (the Childe of Hale), who reputedly was a 9ft 3in giant who lived in Hale during the late fifteenth century. His gravestone can be visited on the south side of the church. The church interior has some fine examples of eighteenth-century architecture.

Hale lighthouse: Hale lighthouse stands at the tip of Hale Head, the southernmost point of the north Mersey shore. It was from here that Prince Rupert crossed the Mersey with his soldiers. The lighthouse is no longer functional.

The Macclesfield Canal

START Nelson Pit car park, Higher
Poynton, SK12 1TH, GR SJ944 834

DISTANCE 3 miles (5km)
or 5 miles (8km)

MAPS OS Landranger 109
Manchester, Bolton & Warrington and
OS Landranger 118 Stoke-on-Trent
& Macclesfield; OS Explorer 268
Wilmslow, Macclesfield & Congleton

WHERE TO EAT AND DRINK
Lyme Breeze at bridge 18 of the
Macclesfield Canal, To1625 871120;
Bailey's Trading Post at bridge 15 of
the canal, To1625 872277; The Miners
Arms, Adlington, To1625 872731,
just off the route; The Boar's Head,
To1625 876676, close to the start

An old canal and an old railway.

① From the car park start at Nelson Pit, walk through towards the back
of the car park directly onto the Macclesfield Canal towpath and turn
right, walking under bridges 15, 16 and 17, past the marina to bridge 18.
The short walk goes up onto the road here. Turn right, soon crossing a
bridge over the old railway. Refreshments are available by continuing to
the crossroads and turning right to reach the Miners Arms. The walk
rejoins the longer route by dropping down onto the railway track bed,
which is used by the Middlewood Way.

② The longer route continues along the towpath. Go under bridge 19,
leading to Woodend Farm, where power lines cross the canal. Continue
along the towpath to reach road bridge 21. Go up to the road and turn
left, travelling over a bridge but dropping immediately down onto the
Middlewood Way. Follow the trackbed to reach the shorter route near
Wood Lanes. To reach the Miners Arms leave the trackbed at the road and
follow the directions above.

From Wood Lanes continue along the Middlewood Way, passing the
Poynton Coppice car park and picnic area to the left. At road bridge 15
leave the trackbed and climb to the road. The car park is at the bridge top.
The Boar's Head Inn can be seen on the other side of the bridge.

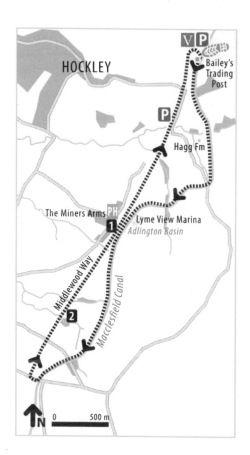

Points of interest

Macclesfield Canal: Construction began in 1826, after the enabling Act of Parliament, and took 5 years. The canal is 28 miles long, linking the Peak Forest Canal at Marple to the Trent and Mersey at Hardings Wood Junction. It is, therefore, part of the system known as the Cheshire Ring. After years of decline, restoration began in the 1960s.

Middlewood Way: The local industries – silk, coal and stone as well as the more famous cotton mills – were served by the Canal until the coming of the railways. This line, the Macclesfield, Bollington and Marple, was just 10 miles long, and spent its life on an economic knife-edge. It was closed in 1970. The local councils that border the line have restored it as a walk and cycle track (and, for part of its length, a bridleway) all the way from Macclesfield to Marple.

Maiden Castle

START Maiden Castle car park, GR SJ494 526

DISTANCE 3 miles (5km)

MAPS OS Explorer 257 Crewe & Nantwich

WHERE TO EAT AND DRINK
The Sandstone, Nantwich Rd (A534), To1829 782333; The Bickerton Poacher, Bulkeley To1829 720226

This moderate walk explores some of the features of Bickerton Hill and takes in Maiden Castle; there are great views across the north Cheshire and Welsh countryside.

1 Turn left at the entrance to the car park and go uphill on the Sandstone Trail. At the top of the hill is a crossroad of paths. Take the right-hand one, which continues upwards and becomes a series of steps. At the top is an entrance to Maiden Castle Iron Age Fort. On a clear day it is possible to see across the village of Brown Knowl to the two Liverpool cathedrals to the north-west and the Welsh hills. Continue along this path, which eventually declines down a set of steps and onto another crossroad of paths (about 650yds); carry straight on.

2 Shortly the path turns left and continues along the edge of the escarpment. 'Mad Allen's Hole' is close by (although very difficult to find). The whole of the Maiden Castle area is being returned to its lowland heath state through the introduction of Welsh ponies, which graze it during the summer months.

3 Keep going along the woodland path downhill for about 650yds until you reach Goldford La. Turn right and proceed down the lane for about ¾ mile, passing Goldford Farm, Hill Farm and Pool Farm on the left, until there is a track diagonally to the right. There is notice saying 'Private Land No Parking' but there is a right of way up it. Follow the track uphill until a junction is reached. Ahead is a small car park for disabled people and to the left a continuation of the track.

4 Keep on the track for about 200yds, where the track meets a footpath. Turn left downhill and follow the path back to the car park in about ¾ mile. Where the path runs alongside a boundary fence, there are excellent views across south Cheshire and south towards Shropshire.

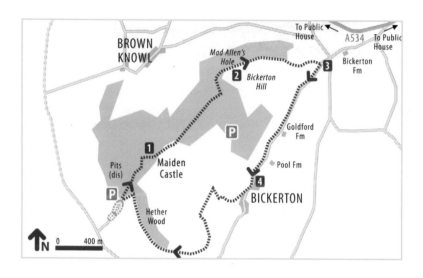

Maiden Castle: An Iron Age hill fort, which was protected by the steep cliff to its west and a double rampart and ditch to the east.

Mad Allen's Hole: It is believed to be the home of a John Harris (eighteenth century), or it could be the home of an eccentric called Mad Allen (nineteenth century).

Nantwich & the River Weaver

START The Crown Hotel, High
St (north side of The Square),
Nantwich, CW5 5AS, GR SJ654 522

DISTANCE 3 miles (5km)
or 4 miles (6.5km)

MAPS OS Landranger 118
Stoke-on-Trent & Macclesfield;
OS Explorer 257 Crewe & Nantwich

WHERE TO EAT AND DRINK
Plenty of places in Nantwich

A walk through Nantwich and on surfaced paths by the river.

1 Turn away from The Square towards Oat Market, passing the Union Inn, an eighteenth-century coaching inn, on the right. Go straight ahead at Wall La, passing between shops, and enter the large car park. Keep to the right side of the road and pass by the modern swimming baths on your left and the Old Outdoor Brine Baths, built in 1883, next to them. At the end of these buildings turn left towards the River Weaver and left again before the footbridge to follow the river back towards the town.

2 Pass under a bridge and up to traffic lights at a further bridge. Turn right, crossing over the bridge into Welsh Row. Go past the Cheshire Cat and continue past Marsh La, which comes in on the left, to Malthouse Cottage, mentioned in late eighteenth-century rating lists. You can now see the Shropshire Union Canal Bridge spanning the road further on, and an extension of the walk can be made from here in that direction to include Dorfold Hall about 800yds further on.

Return back down Welsh Row on the opposite side to the river bridge. Cross over and turn right and right again in 75yds by a paved area to cross the river. Take the middle path of three towards houses ahead, going over another bridge and turning left. Bear half-left to cross a further bridge and go immediately right, under the railway bridge. Bear left along a path to the grave of Lieutenant Brown.

Continue with the path until it comes out through a car park and onto Shrewbridge Rd, and cross over to a drive, which has Brookfield House on the right and a children's playground on the left. The drive narrows as it runs between two houses fronting onto Wellington Rd. In the garden of a house on the left is a small brick building, which used to be a school. Turn left into Wellington Rd, go over the level crossing, then straight ahead over the roundabout into Pillory St.

Halfway down on the left and set back from the road is a chapel of the Society of Friends, now converted into a theatre for the Nantwich Players. Between the chapel and the road was the site of an old town

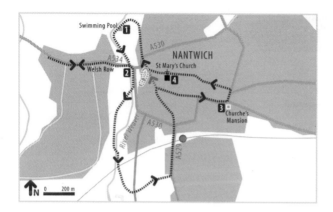

pillory. Nantwich Museum, once the public library, is on the opposite side of the road. Continue for another 150yds along Pillory St and then turn right into Hospital St. About 250yds up on the left is Sweetbriar Hall, a distinctive black and white building.

For the shorter version of the walk, turn left into Church Lane, through St Mary's churchyard, then left again back to the Crown Hotel.

③   As you move away from the town centre, past a mini roundabout, notice some fine old properties, many of which still retain medieval features. By a second, larger roundabout, you will find Churche's Mansion on the right, a fine Elizabethan timber-framed house open to the public.

④   Turn left here along the road to Chester and left again past the Nantwich veterinary hospital, down South Crofts, turning right at the end and then immediately left into Monk's La. On your right are the Dysart Buildings and halfway along on the left is The Bowling Green, where you can get refreshments. Monk's La brings you out on the north side of St Mary's churchyard, and into The Square again. Turn right along the High St back to the Crown Hotel.

Points of interest

Nantwich has an almost entirely Elizabethan centre, the result of a fire that devastated the town in 1538. The fire raged for twenty days; it destroyed all but three of the town's main buildings. Sweetbriar Hall, Churche's Mansion and the parish church of St Mary's were the three survivors, and each is passed on this route. Following the fire, Elizabeth I donated £2,000 and organized a nationwide collection, raising £30,000, a vast sum for the time, to finance the rebuilding of the town.

Raw Head

START Lay-by on the
A534, GR SJ517564

DISTANCE 3 miles (5km)
or 5¾ miles (9km)

MAPS OS Explorer 257
Crewe & Nantwich

WHERE TO EAT AND DRINK
The Pheasant Inn, Higher
Burwardsley, T01829 770434
(walker- and dog-friendly)

A moderate walk over a mix of tracks, roads and paths with some hills.

1 Cross the A534 road and go up Coppermine La. Turn left at a stile in about 150yds. Follow this path until it joins the Sandstone Trail (about 400yds). Turn right past Chiflik Farm and onto a path by the edge of woodland. Follow this path for about 1,000yds, passing 'Musket's Hole' at about 700yds, to Raw Head trigonometry point. Keep on this path for about ¾ mile and turn right at the junction with a track.

2 In about 350yds turn left onto a path. Go across a field and turn right onto a woodland track in about 350yds. Follow this track to Coppermine La in about 350yds, leading downhill to the start point (about ½ mile).

The extended walk begins with a left turn onto a footpath at about 50yds after 2. Follow this path downhill for about ¾ mile over five fields and a stream, in a woodland area, to Sarra La. Turn right for about ¾ mile, passing the Cheshire Workshops.

3 At the junction at the end of the lane take the right fork to Rock La and at the next fork bear right into Hill La. In about 500yds the lane becomes more track-like. In a further 400yds turn right onto a waymarked track and at a gate turn right onto a footpath. Follow this path through the wood for about 600yds, then turn right to a stone wall by a large tree and then left onto a path.

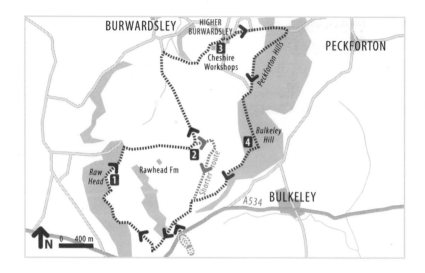

4 In about 400yds turn left and right onto a track (Sandstone Trail). In just over 150yds turn left and climb up a stair of stones. Follow this path to the summit of Bulkeley Hill and along the edge of the hill for about 525yds, until a gate is reached at the edge of the woodland area. Turn left just before the gate and in about 30yds turn right and go through a kissing gate (signposted to the Bickerton Poacher). Take this path and follow it until a gate is reached (600yds). Continue along the track to Coppermine La. Turn left downhill to the start point.

Points of interest

Raw Head trig point: Excellent views.
   Cheshire Workshops, Higher Burwardsley: Candle-making and food and drink.

START Walton Hall Garden pay & display car park, WA4 6SN, GR SJ597 852; alternatively the car park near the Walton Arms

DISTANCE 3 miles (5km)

MAPS OS Landranger 108 Liverpool, Southport & Wigan; OS Explorer 276 Bolton, Wigan & Warrington

WHERE TO EAT AND DRINK Refreshments available at Walton Gardens when open

A pleasant walk along a canal path and country lanes.

1 Leave the car park and descend to the Walton stretch of the Bridgewater Canal via a set of steps. Turn left and follow the canal path alongside the canal until you reach Hough Bridge. Go under the bridge and turn left to walk up to and over Hough Bridge. Continue along Hough La, passing by Beech Tree Farm and Hillfoot Farm.

2 Soon Walton golf course is on both sides, but stay on the lane to reach a T–junction at Appleton Reservoir.

Turn left and walk along Park La to the end of the reservoir, where a set of steps takes you up to the path. Go through the gate and along a well-defined path that skirts the reservoir. Emerge onto a lane and after a few yards immediately turn right to follow the path around the reservoir. Do not turn off onto any side paths, simply follow the path around the reservoir until it meets Park La once more. There is plenty of birdlife to look at on the reservoir and in the reed beds.

At Park La turn left along the road, passing several dwellings with the golf course on your right, to arrive at a crossroads. Turn right here along Warrington Rd, passing the entrance to Walton golf course to reach a canal bridge.

3 At the road junction turn right, and continue along a 'No Through Road' signposted to Walton Hall and Gardens, and return to the car park.

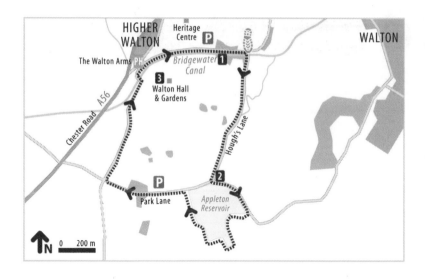

Points of interest

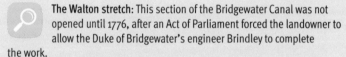

The Walton stretch: This section of the Bridgewater Canal was not opened until 1776, after an Act of Parliament forced the landowner to allow the Duke of Bridgewater's engineer Brindley to complete the work.

Walton Gardens: Opened to the public in 1945, these are well worth a visit. Refreshments and toilets available when the grounds are open.

Farndon & the River Dee

START Car park and picnic spot by
the river, Farndon, GR SJ411 544

DISTANCE 3¼ miles (5km)

MAPS OS Explorer 257
Crewe & Nantwich

WHERE TO EAT AND DRINK
Hildegard's Café, Holt, T01829 270750

An easy walk along the River Dee, returning across fields and tracks.

1   With the Dee Bridge to the rear and Farndon Cliffs to the left, take
the right-hand path by the river. In about 50yds the path becomes a
wooden walkway for about 350yds. Take the right-hand path along the
river bank where the track forks. At about 500yds a look to the right
reveals Holt Castle on the Holt side of the river, and at about ¾ mile the
path passes under the A534. In about 600yds take a left turn at a field
boundary. At the time of the survey the path across the field had been
ploughed up, but the line of the path could be judged by the alignment of
three trees that pointed to a waymarked track.

2   Cross the field and join the start of a rough track for about 880yds;
turn left just before Crewe Hall Farm. Follow the path northwards over six
fields for about 1,000yds to a junction with the A534 road. Take a left turn
just before the road down a parallel track (old road) for about 300yds and
turn right under the road bridge. Follow this track for about 500yds and
take a left turn shortly onto a wooden walkway with the Dee Cliffs to the
right. This walkway leads directly back to the car park by the Dee Bridge.

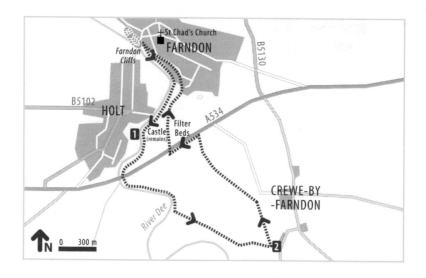

Points of interest

🔍 **Dee Bridge/Farndon Cliffs:** Triassic rock sequence showing the desert-like conditions at that time.

   Holt Castle: Rather derelict now, but thought to have been built to guard the river crossing. Built in 1282 to 1311. Other names are Chastellion or Castrum Leonis – The Lion Castle.

   St Chad's church: Interest lies in the different building styles resulting from its long history, and damage inflicted on it during the Civil War.

Start The crossroads, Adlington, GR SJ911 804

Distance 3½ miles (5.5km)

Maps OS Landranger 109 Manchester, Bolton & Warrington; OS Explorer 268 Wilmslow, Macclesfield & Congleton

Where to eat and drink The Legh Arms Inn, Adlington, T01625 829211

A pleasant walk, with an extension to a superb hall.

From the crossroads – the junction of the A523 and Brookledge La in Adlington – walk through the village east, away from the main road, past the Legh Arms Inn and over the railway. After approximately 300yds turn right into Wych La. Walk down but continue straight ahead where Wych La junctions with Broughton La.

① Walk down a tarmac drive, beside a wood; continue with it as it bears left, away from the wood, but where it turns sharply right, go left, over a stile, and cross the field beyond to reach Harrop Green Farm. Go through the farmyard and along a track to a path marker post. Go over, turn right and walk with the hedge on the right across to a marker post where the path bears left across to an oak, over a stile and then gradually uphill to the left-hand corner of the field. This takes you out onto the Middlewood Way.

② Turn right along the old railway trackbed for about 600yds, past Higher Doles Farm to a small flight of steps leading up to a metal kissing gate. Go through, turn left and walk to a property called 'Whiteley Croft'. Bear right here and continue along a track through a gate, and follow the marker post to a stile in the hedge. Go over and continue to cross a footbridge. Go half-right to reach a stile. Go over and walk ahead to reach another stile. Go over and, keeping a house and hedge on the right, continue across a field and under a power line to reach a stile in the field corner. Go over, turn left and follow the hedge to a plank bridge. Cross this and the stile beyond, then turn right along a hedge. Go through a gate and across a rough field, dropping down to another gate leading onto Wych La. Turn right along the lane, crossing a stream to return to the outward route. Now reverse the route back into Adlington.

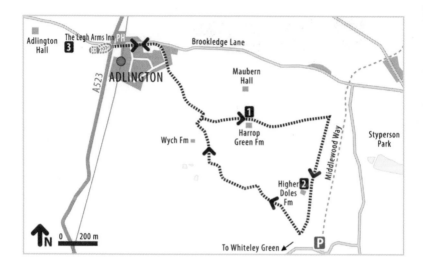

③ The extension of the walk crosses the A523, with care, and follows the road opposite to reach, to the left, Adlington Hall. Return along the same route. This extension adds about 1¼ miles to the route.

Points of interest

Middlewood Way: See note to Walks 8 & 9.

Adlington Hall: Although the Hall has been in the hands of the Legh family since 1315, the oldest part of the building that now occupies the site dates from the fifteenth century. The black-and-white 'Cheshire' style – the oldest part – includes an early sixteenth-century Great Hall with a fine hammerbeam ceiling. The later, brick addition to the house is Georgian. One room in the Hall houses an organ said to have been played by Handel. The Hall stands in parkland that was the work of Capability Brown.

Alvanley & Helsby

START Helsby Quarry Local Nature Reserve car park, GR SJ489 749

DISTANCE 3½ miles (5.5km)

MAPS OS Landranger 117 Chester & Wrexham; OS Explorer 267 Northwich & Delamere Forest

WHERE TO EAT AND DRINK The Bull's Head, Frodsham, T01928 733761; The Ring O' Bells, Frodsham, T01928 732068 (both opposite Overton church)

A walk with beautiful views.

① Leave the car park and cross over the road to Hill Rd South. Follow it to a facing gate, then onto the National Trust property of Helsby Hill, following a path that climbs through trees. After about 100yds, where the path bears right between outcrops of rock, go forward, crossing onto a rough track. Continue past a pond and Harmers Lake Farm to reach a metalled lane. After Firs farmhouse on your right, the road bears left passing trees. Just before reaching a white cottage to the right, take a footpath on the right that is signed 'Tarvin Road and Commonside'.

Go over a stile and cross a field, keeping to the left edge. Go over wooden steps and stay to the left to cross another stile. Skirt the left edge of the next field and turn right at a facing fence. Go ahead to reach a stile on your left and go over onto a track that descends to a road.

② Go left, passing Tuehill House on your left, and carry on down the road turning right into The Ridgeway, walking past Fox Hill Farm and Burrows La on your right to reach the Ridgeway Caravan Park on your left. Opposite is a small wood; take the steps that lead into it, continuing on a well-defined track that descends left and follows a stream. Cross the stream at a small wooden bridge and bear left to skirt a field. Keeping a small wood to your left, continue to a stile. Go over and keep left. Descend wooden steps on your left, go over a stile and follow a track across a field. Go over another stile onto a road.

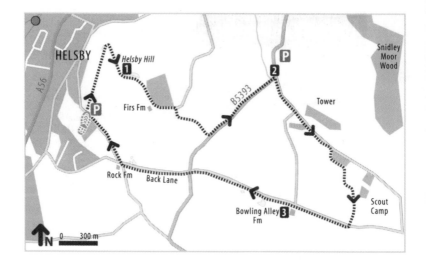

3 Go right down the road, passing Cliff Farm House on your left, to reach Bowling Alley Farm. Continue past dwellings and a small farm on your left to arrive at a crossroads. Go over and continue walking down Back La. At a second crossroads go right, passing dwellings on both sides of the road back to the car park.

Points of interest

Helsby Hill: In the latter part of the eighteenth century the mail was carried on horseback from Chester to Warrington via Helsby. A highwayman who robbed the mailman and was eventually caught in Exeter stood trial at Chester in 1795 and was gibbeted near the scene of his crime on Helsby Hill.

Around Church Minshull

START Near the Badger Inn, Church Minshull, CW5 6DY, GR SJ665 605

DISTANCE 3½ miles (5.5km) or 4½ miles (7km)

MAPS OS Landranger 118 Stoke-on-Trent & Macclesfield; OS Explorer 267 Northwich & Delamere Forest

WHERE TO EAT AND DRINK The Badger Inn, Minshull (an eighteenth-century coaching inn of historic and architectural interest), T01270 522348

An easy and charming walk with plenty of architectural interest.

1 Walk a short way north towards the church and turn right on the road to Crewe. Go over the River Weaver and walk a short distance to reach the Shropshire Union Canal. Turn left along the towpath for approximately 1¼ miles to reach Weaver Bank Bridge, bridge 19. Wimboldsley Hall and the Verdin Arms are on your right along a public footpath, and the main London–Glasgow railway is directly ahead.

2 At Weaver Bank Bridge go up through a gate and turn right, away from Wimboldsley Hall, towards woodland. Follow the right-hand edge of the wood, cutting across at an obvious point. Continue round over stiles and follow a long finger of woodland to go down to meet the River Weaver again. With the river on your left, proceed 100yds, going left over a wide footbridge across the river, and head directly up to meet a delightful green lane. Continue along the lane until it becomes metalled, continuing for another ½ mile or so to reach Lea Green Hall Farm.

3 A footpath goes through the farmyard and exits at the rear of the yard. The exit is just before the last barn. Bear right across to a wood. Drop down through the woodland, following the marker posts to the river. Go right and follow the bank until the wood ends. Continue along a field boundary on your right to reach a road. Go left along the road back to the start point.

An alternative route from Lea Green Hall is to continue along the lane to meet the road. Again go left to reach the start point. This alternative is about 1 mile longer.

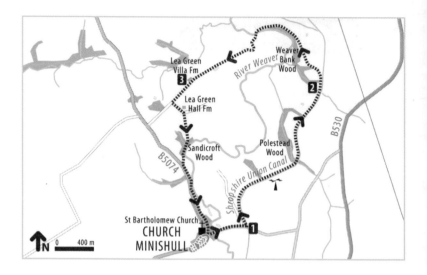

Points of interest

The parish church of St Bartholomew, Church Minshull, was commissioned in 1702 and paid for by an extraordinary rate levied on the parishioners. The church contains the vault of the Wades of Wades Green, who may have connections with Field Marshal Wade of Jacobite fame.

The Bollin & Morley

START Car park on the B5166
in Wilmslow, GR SJ840 822

DISTANCE 3½ miles (5.5km)

MAPS OS Landranger
109 Manchester, Bolton &
Warrington; OS Explorer 268
Wilmslow, Macclesfield & Congleton

WHERE TO EAT AND DRINK
The Mill Kitchen, Quarry Bank
Mill (same opening hours as
the mill); there are cafés, pubs
and restaurants in Wilmslow

An easy walk on well-maintained tracks. It can be combined with a visit to Styal, which is well worthwhile.

From the car park follow the tarmac path heading north, with the River Bollin on your left and the toilets on your right, to cross Twinnies Bridge beside the road and enter the National Trust area on your left.

1 Now simply keep to the path with the river still on your left all the way to Quarry Bank Mill. (See the National Trust map at Twinnies Bridge for details, as these paths are concessionary and many do not appear on the OS map.)

2 Keep on the main tarmac track through the mill buildings and then look for a signpost saying 'Footpath to Morley' on the left. The sign indicates you follow an old cobbled packhorse road, leading down, over the river, and straight ahead to Bank House Farm. The main part of Styal Country Park is to the right here. Walk ahead with gardens to the right and left. Go forwards through the farmyard and down the farm road to the main road, where you turn right and then left at the first junction, signposted 'Morley Green and Mobberley' (take care as this is a busy road).

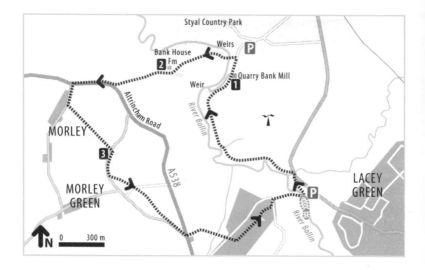

③ After 100yds turn left at a lane passing 'Chelsea Cottages'. Passing a garage on the right side, enter a field by a stile and bear left to another stile 15yds to the left of a large tree, then ahead to a further stile and a minor road. Turn right here and follow the road for 200yds, then go left opposite Moss Grove Farm down a grassy track. At a crossing of tracks carry straight on eventually to join a road, then turn left and keep 100yds ahead to the busy road once more (A538).

Cross this road and keep straight ahead down a path opposite, signposted to 'Kings Road and Twinnies Bridge'. Ignore the next signpost for Twinnies Bridge and keep straight ahead over a bridge. Turn left to Pownall Hall Farm. Walk along a track behind houses with fenced-off gardens either side. Continue straight along this track and then left at the road and right down a bridlepath just before you reach the rugby club. Follow this bridlepath back to the car park.

Points of interest

Quarry Bank Mill: Founded in 1784 as a water-powered cotton spinning mill, it is now run as a working museum and is open to the public (summer 11am–6pm; winter 11am–5pm, closed Mon).
Styal Country Park: Woodland walks through the park, including the Apprentices Walk via Twinnies Bridge and Wilmslow. The estate, built for mill owners and workers, belongs to the National Trust (open to the public).

Eccleston & Eaton Hall

START Eccleston church,
CH4 9HD, GR SJ413 626

DISTANCE 3½ miles (5.5km)

MAPS OS Landranger 117
Chester & Wrexham; OS Explorer
266 Wirral & Chester

WHERE TO EAT AND DRINK
Nowhere on the route, but plenty of
places in nearby Chester or at Aldford
(where the parking is easier), a mile
to the south of the iron bridge

A fine river and an elegant stately home.

Please note that the walk through the grounds of Eaton Hall is only open to the
public on certain days of the year. Check the website www.eatonhall.co.uk for
details of opening times. At other times the walk along the Dee from Eccleston
to the iron bridge can still be followed. The best return is then back along the
same route.

1 From the church go eastwards for 50yds down to a gate, going
through a gateway and along the track to reach the left bank of the River
Dee. Turn right along the riverbank, soon reaching a point where a lane
reaches the bank. Opposite here another track leads away from the water.
The clue to the existence of these apparently useless tracks is in the name
of the farm on the opposite bank. That is Ferry Farm, the tracks once
being linked by a ferry.

2 Now continue along the river. The track that is approached, to the
right, as the river bears right is the Old Roman road heading southward
from *Deva* (Chester). Go down steps and continue to reach Eaton Stud.
Beyond the Stud, the river bends away to the right, heading towards
the horseshoe bend of Crook of Dee. The path does not follow the river
around the Crook, but instead goes right, through a gate, and through a
beautiful woodland (which is a particular delight in spring). Go past a
cottage to reach the Dee again and continue along the riverbank to reach
an ornate iron bridge.

3 If Eaton Hall is open, turn right at the bridge, following the track
through the park, passing the Hall to the right. Beyond the Hall the track
bears right, then left, following the Roman road close to the river and the
outward route. Continue along the track back into Eccleston, emerging
opposite the church.

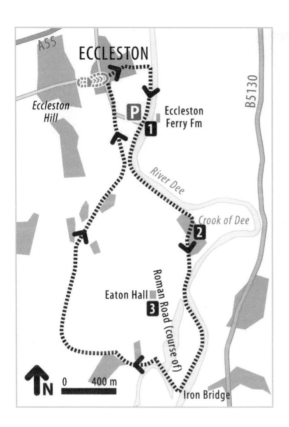

Points of interest

River Dee: The Dee is an exceptional river, beautiful for virtually its entire length. It flows past Llangollen, where it creates one of Britain's best slalom canoe courses, and close to the estate of Owain Glyndwr, who led the last Welsh rebellion against the English. It flows around Chester.

Eaton Hall: This modern, marbled-fenced mansion was built for the Duke of Westminster, who owns a large area of the county to the south of Chester.

Eccleston: The church of St Mary the Virgin is the work of G. F. Bodley, chief architect to the Duke of Westminster. It was built in the last years of the nineteenth century. Inside there are some exquisite carved stones, and memorials to several Dukes of Westminster.

START At the Sandstone Trail car park at Beacon Hill, GR SJ519 766

DISTANCE 3½ miles (5.5km)

MAPS OS Landranger 108 Liverpool, Southport & Wigan; OS Explorer 267 Northwich & Delamere Forest

WHERE TO EAT AND DRINK
The Bull's Head, Frodsham, T01928 733761; The Ring O' Bells, Frodsham, T01928 732068 (both inns opposite Overton church)

A walk along part of the Sandstone Trail with extensive views.

Leave the car park and turn right, then after 100yds turn left onto the Sandstone Trail. Walk down, emerging onto a golf course, and follow the yellow Sandstone Trail marker posts until reaching a finger-post as you enter woods. Go down steps ahead and bear left (beware unfenced cliffs), going down metal steps at 'Bakers Dozen' and continuing to the next finger-post.

[1] Follow the one directing you along the Sandstone Trail, reaching stone steps carved in the rock face. With the golf course on your left, walk along following the trail and passing a view point with views over the Mersey, Liverpool and towards Wales. Just past this, a finger-post points left along the Sandstone Trail; follow it up some steps and at the top walk 50yds to a yellow post and turn right, then almost immediately left, and follow for 300yds to another finger-post in the woods. Ignore and carry on ahead with the field on your left, going up some steps. Ignoring a right of way on the right, carry straight on, reaching a metal gate. Go through and continue to a road crossing over and up a footpath opposite.

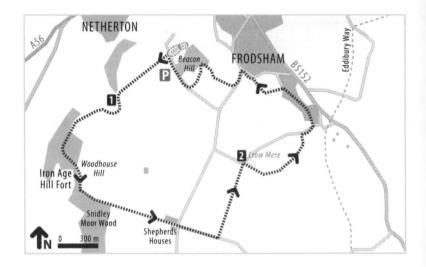

②   On reaching the next lane, turn left and walk to a junction at Crowmere Lake. Turn right beside the lake and follow the track around past a property on the left. After a short distance the track bends to the left and the path carries on through trees and down through Marl Pits, with extensive views to the east across the Cheshire Plain and the Peak District.

At the metal gate turn right and right again onto a lane. After 100yds turn left onto Top Rd and follow to a bend in the road where there is a metal gate leading into a meadow and play area. Go through, keeping the hedge on your right for 200yds, then go over a metal ladder stile in the hedge on the right. Walk down one field through a gap in a fence, go straight ahead and after 200yds climb over another metal ladder stile onto a lane. Turn left and walk 150yds to a junction; turn left, walking 150yds to another lane on your right. Follow this around past one property to a second house and bear left, passing through stone gates marked Delamere Way. Continue to another lane and turn right, walking uphill back to the car park.

Points of interest

Iron Age hill fort, Woodhouse Hill: Roughly 4½ acres of hilltop are encircled by stone-faced ramparts, which advanced dating techniques suggest were originally built during the Late Bronze Age.

Moore Nature Reserve

START Moore Nature Reserve
car park, GR SJ578 855

DISTANCE 3½ miles (5.5km)

MAPS OS Landranger 108 Liverpool,
Southport & Wigan; OS Explorer
276 Bolton, Wigan & Warrington

WHERE TO EAT AND DRINK
The Red Lion, Runcorn Rd,
Moore, 01925 740205

A short walk through an attractive nature reserve.

1   Leaving the car at the reserve's entrance, turn right and for the
next mile keep to a wide circular track, which you follow, ignoring all side
paths and keeping to the left. It eventually returns to the swing bridge
over the Manchester Ship Canal. Cross over the bridge and turn right into
Promenade Rd immediately after crossing; follow the road for ¾ mile as
it gently ascends back over the railway and to the junction of Moss La and
Runcorn Rd.

2   The Red Lion is a short walk to the right down Runcorn Rd; however,
turn left and walk along the pavement up to the Bridgewater Canal. Go
through the gap onto the towpath, turn left and walk for some 700yds
along the canal. Rejoin the main road again where a gap appears, turning
right opposite the village shop. Cross the road, with care, and walk past
the Methodist church.

3   Turn left after 50yds into Moore La and follow it for 400yds as it
gradually descends to the Moore Lane swing bridge. The bridge provides
fine views to the high-level Stockton Bridge upriver. Walk over the bridge
back to the start.

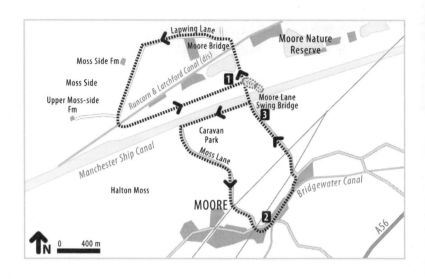

Points of interest

Moore Lane swing bridge: This was one of the last motor-driven bridges to be constructed over the Manchester Ship Canal and remains one of the last still in operation. It was featured, briefly, in the Oscar-winning film *Yanks*, which starred Richard Gere.

START The National Trust car park in Styal, GR SJ836 836

DISTANCE 3½ miles (5.5km)

MAPS OS Landranger 109 Manchester, Bolton & Warrington; OS Explorer 268 Wilmslow, Macclesfield & Congleton

WHERE TO EAT AND DRINK
The Ship Inn, Styal, T01625 444888; The Mill Kitchen, Quarry Bank Mill

An easy walk, with a couple of short climbs, through farmland and a beautiful wooded valley. Muddy after rain.

Leave the car park by the footpath in the bottom right corner. Then turn left alongside some cottages that are part of the Styal Model Village. At the end of the first row of cottages turn left, passing the old village cross, onto the footpath signposted Quarry Bank Mill. Keep straight ahead at a rough track and when you reach a metalled road cross and turn right along a footpath which skirts the car park. Go around the edge of the car park and leave through two gates into a field.

Follow a well trodden path through several fields, and where the footpath descends over cobbles you reach a gate. Go through and down a grassy bank to the right to a gate. This returns to National Trust property and leads through splendidly attractive woodland. Down on the left is the River Bollin and the path leads all the way to the mill.

1 After passing the mill pond to the left, and a play area, the path enters the mill grounds. The large building is Quarry Bank Mill (see note to Walk 21) and refreshments are available here in the café. To continue the walk, climb steadily uphill along the road with the mill on your left. Take a footpath on the left signposted 'To the woods'. Take care on the cobbles, which can be slippery when wet.

2 After crossing a rough track, turn left at a path junction (signposted 'woods'). This drops steeply; walk down to the left to descend to the River Bollin, gully on your right. Turn right here along the river bank.
    The footpath now follows the river around a big loop. 100yds after passing a footbridge across the Bollin, leave the river and take a path steeply uphill. This eventually levels out and contours above another steep gully. When you reach a barrier, turn right down some steps, descending

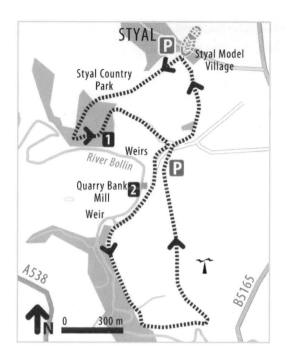

into the gully and eventually crossing it by a stone bridge. Climb some steps on the other side, bearing left by another barrier, then climb steadily, emerging out of the woods through a 'pinch' gap in the wall. Go straight across a rough track here. The footpath beyond leads past a chapel onto a cobbled road. Keep straight ahead into the main street of Styal. Refreshments are to the right at The Ship Inn, or turn left to return to the car park.

Points of interest

Styal Model Village: Styal was built in the 1820s by enlightened mill owner Samuel Greg to house his expanding workforce. Greg was concerned that his employees should live close to the mill and in an attractive environment, so he built several terraces of picturesque cottages, together with a church, shop and school. Although the village shop is no longer in business, there is an interesting display of the products which would have been sold there at the turn of the century.

START Car park behind the
British Legion Club, Tarporley,
CW6 0DZ, GR SJ554 624

DISTANCE 3½ miles (5.5km)

MAPS OS Landranger 108 Liverpool,
Southport & Wigan; OS Explorer
276 Bolton, Wigan & Warrington

WHERE TO EAT AND DRINK Various
places in Tarporley including The
Swan Inn, To1829 733838; The Shady
Oak, To1829 730581, near Tarporley

A walk on old bridleways through typical Cheshire country and beside the
Shropshire Union Canal.

Leave the car park and turn right up the High St. Just after the police
station turn left to reach the lychgate of St Helen's church. Go through a
gate and follow the edge of the churchyard to the kissing gate. Follow the
path beyond, bearing right beneath the telegraph poles. Walk towards a
hedge on your right with a house beyond.

1 Cross a stile by the gate and walk past a pond and a house. The track
bears right along the bypass. Walk 300yds along the track to a gate on the
right and cross the busy A49 bypass.

On the other side, a sign reads 'To Sandstone Trail, Iddenshall'.
The way may be obscured by undergrowth, but look for a stile on the
left, 10yds from the roadside. Cross this, turn right and walk between
two hedges. After 150yds you will reach a house on the right. Bear left
down the track. About 100yds from the house turn right through a gap
in the hedge and walk along this pleasant bridleway, which drops gently
downhill. You will eventually reach a signpost for the Sandstone Trail.

Continue in the direction of Beeston Castle and Bulkeley Hill. Cross
a double stile and follow a fence on the left. Beeston Castle can be seen
ahead. Walk in the general direction of the castle, crossing several stiles.
The seventh stile leads to a junction of lanes. Go down the facing lane and
through a metal kissing gate on the right. Keep the boundary on your left,
pass over a wooden bridge to another metal kissing gate, through a field
and another metal gate before emerging onto a lane.

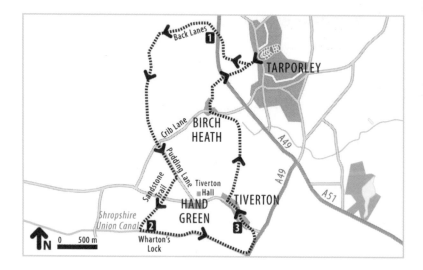

[2] Cross this and continue with the hedge on your right until you reach the Shropshire Union Canal (see note to Walk 5) at Wharton's Lock. Cross the canal via the small footbridge above the lower lock chamber, turn left and follow the towpath. (If you were to turn right here you would quickly reach The Shady Oak.) After about 1 mile you will reach the road bridge for the A49.

[3] Climb to the road here and turn left, then left again into Tiverton. Carry on walking past a telephone box and monument on the left to reach a cluster of houses on the right called 'The Dale'. Turn right down the signposted footpath, walking between two earth banks and beneath a canopy of hawthorns. The bridleway ends at a metal gate into a large field. Go over and cross the field towards a telegraph pole by a tree in the distant corner. At a set of stiles where three paths meet, bear left. Cross the next stile and follow a track to Birch Heath. Turn between two houses to reach a lane. Just before the farm, turn right along a signposted track; 50yds along cross a stile on the right and bear left across two fields to a stile by a gate. Turn sharp right and, keeping the hedge on your right, walk down to a stile over to the main A49 road. Cross over and the facing stile also and follow the hedge on your left to the first hawthorn tree. Cross the stile here and walk to the church, then retrace your steps back to the start.

Vale Royal

START St Mary's church,
Whitegate, GR SJ629 694

DISTANCE 3½ miles (5.5km)

MAPS OS Landranger 118 Stoke-on-Trent & Macclesfield; OS Explorer 267 Northwich & Delamere Forest

WHERE TO EAT AND DRINK
Nowhere on the route, but refreshments available at the Plough Inn, in nearby Foxwist Green, 01606 889455

A short walk close to one of Cheshire's most historically interesting sites.

1 From the church follow the beautiful, tree-lined drive towards Vale Royal House, but leave it after about 500yds to turn left into a cul-de-sac called St Mary's Drive. Bear right to a road junction, going straight ahead at a footpath signpost to the Vale Royal Golf Club. Follow the yellow marker posts to Rookery Wood and follow the path through. When the edge of the wood is reached, go half-right and cross a field to a gate. Go over onto a path and follow it to its junction with a track.

2 Go right, along the track, for about 300yds to reach a gate; turn along a path on the left marked by a green footpath sign, following the old course of the River Weaver. The path maintains direction beside the meandering river to reach a stile. Go over and continue following the river to a stile on the wood's edge.

3 Turn right and cross the field, bearing right towards a woodland. Carry on, keeping the hedge on your right, to a ladder stile on the right. Go over, bearing left to another ladder stile. Go over and turn right and follow the path around into woodlands. Where the wood edge ends, turn right and cross the field to a stile. Go over onto the drive of Vale Royal House and turn left to reverse the outward route back to Whitegate.

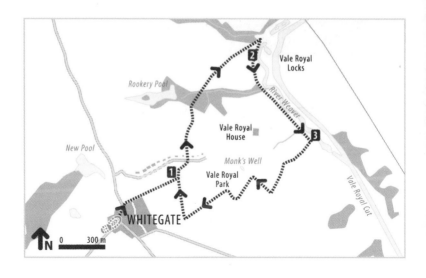

Points of interest

Vale Royal House: Sailing home from a Crusade to the Holy Land, Prince Edward (later Edward I), the Earl of Chester, and his army were caught in a violent storm. Fearing for his life, the prince roared to God that if he were spared he would build an abbey in Cheshire. Work began on Vale Royal Abbey in 1277. When completed it was the largest Cistercian monastery in England. It was dissolved in 1538, the estate passing to Sir Thomas Holcroft who, it is said, had murdered the last abbot. Over time most of the abbey was demolished. Today only the main door survives, the present house dating from the early seventeenth century, though with later additions and modifications.

Whitegate: St Mary's church was once a chapel of Vale Royal Abbey. Today it is the centrepiece of a picturesque village, which includes some thatched cottages to add to the general charm.

Whitchurch & Wirswall

START Free car park in
Whitchurch, GR SJ545 415

DISTANCE 3½ miles (5.5km)

MAPS OS Landranger 117
Chester & Wrexham; OS Explorer
257 Crewe & Nantwich

WHERE TO EAT AND DRINK
The Lock Tavern, Willeymoor, 01948
663274; lots of places in Whitchurch

An easy walk starting from an ancient market town; mainly on field paths and a
stretch of canal towpath.

From the car park head north into Whitchurch town centre, past Tesco's
and uphill past the Civic Centre and impressive church on the hill,
carrying on down to a roundabout with a Sainsbury's on the right. Go
ahead along the B5476 for 400yds to a footpath on the left just before
a postbox. After 150yds a stile on the right takes you across a field to
another. Turn left, coming to a short bridge across a stream and go over,
walking 150yds to the busy A41 road. Cross over with care.

1️⃣ Pass over a stile towards a telegraph pole and, keeping the hedge
on your right, walk to the next stile. Go over several more fields and
stiles, keeping straight ahead at a footpath junction, until you reach the
Shropshire Union Canal.

2️⃣ Cross over the canal bridge and turn right onto the towpath for
1 mile to Willeymoor Lock. Go over the canal, walking on a path beside
a lane to reach the A49. Cross with care and walk up Bradley Green La.
Where the road forks, continue on, following the sign for Bishop Bennet
Way. Go through a gate and follow a rough track. Go through a gate where
a finger-post directs you to Wirswall. Follow the track to a lane where
there is an information board about the Bishop Bennet Way.

3️⃣ Turn left and after 200yds follow the path on the right next to a pair
of double gates. After just 30yds cross over a stile on your right. Follow a
line of telegraph poles through a field to a gate. Keep the hedge on your
right and walk to a set of double gates, going through the left one. Keeping
the boundary on your right, cross to a stile and then over to another.
This is followed by three metal kissing gates, which bring you onto a golf
course. Head towards a line of trees and follow the yellow marker posts

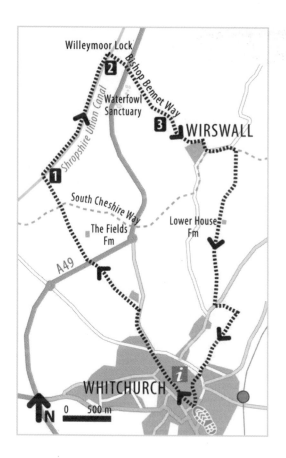

to a lane, coming out almost opposite White Cottage. Aim for the path beside White Cottage and cross a field to a bridge over a disused railway. Go through a metal kissing gate and across two fields, which eventually emerge onto Prince William Cl. Turn right into Elizabeth St. Walk down and go through a recreational ground to the main road; cross over and down a side street towards the town centre. Directly opposite is access back to the car park.

Points of interest

Whitchurch: This ancient market town on the Welsh border is actually in north Shropshire, but close to the Cheshire border.

Wybunbury Moss

START Car park near the church,
Wybunbury, GR SJ969 498

DISTANCE 3½ miles (5.5km)

MAPS OS Explorer 257
Crewe & Nantwich

WHERE TO EAT AND DRINK
The Swan Inn, T01270 841280;
The Red Lion, 01270 841261,
both in Wybunbury

An easy walk around Wybunbury Moss, including a small section of the Moss,
and over fields back to Wybunbury via the church tower.

Exit the car park to the main road and turn right for about 150yds, then
turn left into Kiln La and walk along it to a gate and stile on the left. Go
over the stile and proceed along the footpath with the hedge on the left for
about 650yds. At about 250yds the path crosses a garden of a large house
– follow the signs. There are views of Wybunbury Moss to the right. At
the end of this section turn right onto a track. There are signs and notice
boards for the Moss at this point.

1️⃣ Continue along this track for about 850yds, when the track turns left.
Keep to the right and join a footpath ahead. In about 300yds the path joins
another path at a T–junction. Turn right and shortly turn right and over a
stile into the Moss itself (take note of the notices). Follow the track around
the Moss, which emerges back onto a path. Turn left and follow this path,
keeping to the right past a rubble dump. Then go over a stile and continue
diagonally over two fields.

2️⃣ Enter a new field via a stile and keep to the left by the small lake. At
the end of the lake turn right across the field for about 150yds and turn
right onto a path by the remnants of a field hedge. Follow this path for
about 450yds, passing a building to the right and where the path changes
into a track. Then continue a further 200yds and go ahead when the track
turns to the left. This path ends shortly at a set of steps that exit into the
churchyard. Go past the church tower, which is all that remains of the old
church, and exit onto the main road by the lych gate. Go past the Swan
Inn on the right. Continue along the road back to the car park in about
300yds.

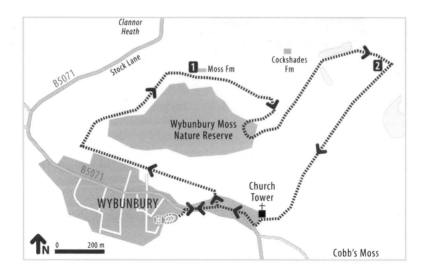

Points of interest

🔍 **Wybunbury Moss Nature Reserve:** A rare example of a floating peat bog (42ft deep); noted for its plant life and invertebrates.

Wybunbury church tower (St Chad's): Only the tower remains. It used to lean to the north but has been straightened using the same methods applied to the Leaning Tower of Pisa.

Acton to Swanley

Flat, easy walking, partly along quiet lanes and the canal.

Turn right after leaving the car park and right again onto the A51. Go past the Star Inn on your right to reach a gravel lane with a waymarker post.

1 This bridleway is about 1 mile long and to the left of it lies Dorfold Hall, while Beeston Hills can be seen in the opposite direction.

2 Turn right on reaching a lane. This is Dig La and you follow it, going over at the crossroads after ½ mile and reaching another crossroads ¼ mile further on at Stoneley Green. Carry straight on past houses until the lane turns right onto a track. Go over a stile, continuing on the track until you see another stile straight ahead.

3 Go over and through a short section of meadows to reach the canal. Turn right onto the canal and follow the towpath, passing under one bridge and reaching a second, where you leave the canal at Swanley.

4 Coming up onto a lane, bear left onto Swanley La and walk ahead a few yards. On the right, between some houses and a plantation, is a stile taking you into a field. Go over and through the field and over another stile onto a private driveway. Cross over to another stile and cross two further fields to a lane. Looking to the left you will see a windmill with a wind pump on top and, a little to the right, St Mary's church, Acton. Go directly over and along a track at Madam's Farm, walking beside the garden and coming out into a large field behind it. Continue over this and through one more field until you reach the track where you turn left to return to Acton village, past the Star Inn and the start.

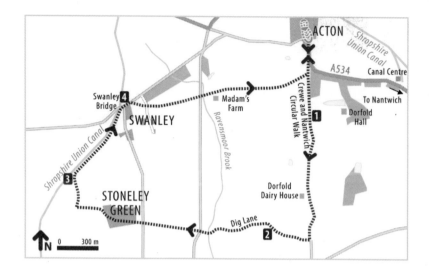

Points of interest

Dorfold Hall: Built in 1616 by Ralph Wilbraham. The drawing room has a fine Jacobean ceiling. The garden has a Spanish chestnut over 1,000 years old. The hall is open to visitors on Tuesday afternoons and Bank Holiday Mondays only, April–Oct.

Windmill: The brickwork is late eighteenth century and the walls are five bricks thick. It ground corn until the late 1880s. In 1890 the sails were replaced by a wind pump and the mill became a water tower supplying the Dorfold estate.

St Mary's church, Acton: This church dates mainly from the thirteenth and fourteenth centuries. It contains carved stones from the late eleventh century and a twelfth-century font.

START The railway bridge
in Ashley, GR SJ774 843

DISTANCE 4 miles (6.5km)

MAPS OS Landranger 109
Manchester, Bolton & Warrington;
OS Explorer 268 Wilmslow,
Macclesfield & Congleton

WHERE TO EAT AND DRINK
There is an inn at Ashley, also a tea
shop/restaurant in Tatton Park

An old park close to the Manchester border.

1 From the bridge, walk westward along the village road on the pavement, heading towards Rostherne, Knutsford and Tatton Park. Follow the road around a sharp left-hand corner, continuing past Stock Farm to the left, then going around a right-hand corner to reach Birkin Farm, also to the left. Beyond, the road turns sharp left to run alongside Tatton Park. The route leaves the road at the bend by going right through a kissing gate.

Follow the track beyond, which soon bears right and heads directly for the M56. At the motorway it turns left to run alongside the road for about 300yds (keep to the fence, right of the woods) , then goes right on a bridge over the motorway. Beyond, a path threads through some woodland to reach a kissing gate, and turns right to another.

2 Go through onto the lane of Ryecroft Farm, on your left. Turn right along the lane, and ignore a signed path to the left, continuing along the lane. Go past a pond with trees to the right and, further on, go along the edge of another clump of pretty woodland.

3 At the wood's extremity the lane dog-legs right; stay with it to reach a junction of lanes. Turn right here and walk down to a road. Follow the road to a distinctive left bend. The house set on the bend is the North Lodge of the Tatton Park estate.

4 Go straight ahead, following the lane past Ashley Hall, going over the motorway and reaching a T–junction with a road. Turn left to return to the start.

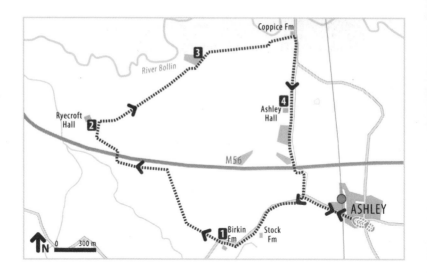

Points of interest

Tatton Park: This superb 1,000-acre park – part deer park, part arboretum with its gardens of trees and shrubs from all over the world – is among the finest in England. It surrounds a house built in the early nineteenth century, but in classical style: its entrance protects a portico supported by vast Corinthian columns. The interior is equally lavish. The earlier mansion of the Egerton family, who owned Tatton until it passed to the National Trust, still stands in the park.

Barthomley & Englesea Brook

START The White Lion, Barthomley, CW2 5PG, GR SJ768 524

DISTANCE 4 miles (6.5km)

MAPS OS Landranger 118 Stoke-on-Trent & Macclesfield; OS Explorer 257 Crewe & Nantwich

WHERE TO EAT AND DRINK The White Lion Inn, Barthomley, T01270 882242

Easy walking, mainly across fields and past an interesting chapel.

Walk down to the road with the pub on your right and turn right at the T–junction. After 25yds turn left up a stony drive, indicated by a waymarker sign on the left and passing Bank cottage. After 100yds and with a bowling green on the left, walk straight ahead into a field following the waymarker posts.

1 The route goes directly ahead across a field to a stile to the right of Churchfield Barns. At the stile turn left and walk past Churchfield Barns on your right along a lane; opposite the buildings is a footpath on the left. Follow this around to a wooden bridge over a stream. Cross and go over a stile onto a lane. Cross over and follow a green lane opposite for ¼ mile to a quiet lane and turn right. Walk ½ mile to a bridge at Englesea Brook. Follow the road as it bends to the left.

2 After a few yards you will pass Englesea Brook Chapel on the left and then walk gradually uphill for 500yds. At a waymarker sign on the left pass through a gap in the hedge and cross several fields, connected by stiles, bearing gradually right until a final stile delivers you onto a quiet lane. Cross over to another stile and go over, crossing two fields. Approximately 100yds after passing a pond on your right is a stile taking you onto a track.

3 Turn left down the track past Mill Dale Farm on the left. The route goes through a gate and down to a pond. Keep to its left, going around until you reach a footpath junction. Follow the waymarker on the left, going up through a coppice and emerging out into a field. Keep straight ahead, going across several fields with stiles. Eventually Barthomley church comes into view. Still keeping ahead, cross over the last field before the church and head for the church, finding a stile. Go over and follow the track to the left past a pond to the church and road. Turn right back to the start.

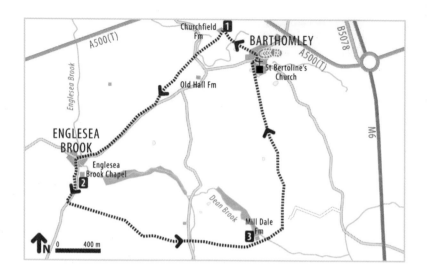

Points of interest

🔍 **Englesea Brook Chapel:** Erected in 1828 and extended to its present size in 1832.

St Bertoline's church, Barthomley: Dedicated to St Bertoline, an eighth-century prince who became a hermit after the loss of his young wife. It was the scene of a massacre in the Civil War, when men fled into the church steeple and were almost stifled by the enemy burning the brushes, mats and forms. They were granted quarter but were later brutally murdered.

START The Sessions House in
Daresbury, WA4 4AJ, GR SJ579 828

DISTANCE 4 miles (6.5km)

MAPS OS Landranger 108
Liverpool, Southport & Wigan

WHERE TO EAT AND DRINK
The Ring O' Bells, Chester Rd,
Daresbury, T01925 740256; The
Hatton Arms, Warrington Rd,
Hatton, T01925 730314

A walk along old country lanes near one of Cheshire's most historic villages.

Turn south from the Sessions House (away from the pub) and walk up the
lane for 500yds. Turn right at a footpath sign, and cross a field to reach a
stile. Cross the busy A56 road with care, and go over another stile on the
opposite side of the road.

1 Follow the footpath for another 250yds to the Daresbury Firs
plantation. The footpath descends steeply through the plantation to reach
a stile; follow the footpath for another 150yds to Delph La. Turn left and
walk up the lane to the A56 once more. Cross the road with caution and
turn right at the second junction ahead, away from the A56.

2 Follow this lane for 70yds and turn left into Newton La, staying
on the lane for ¾ mile until the junction – you will pass over the M56.
Turn left at the junction and follow this lane for 1 mile to the junction
of Pilmoss La – the M56 runs close by to the left and road noise will be
noticeable.

3 Turn left, following the road over the M56 again, continuing along
the lane and keeping left into the village at Hatton. Walk around the sharp
bends to reach the Hatton Arms and village shop. Turn left at the pub into
Daresbury La and walk for 1 mile back into the village of Daresbury. All
Saints parish church is the first building to appear on your right as you
re-enter the village, and 70yds beyond the church is the Sessions House,
where the walk started.

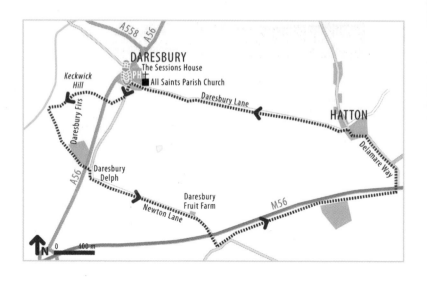

Points of interest

All Saints parish church, Daresbury: A fine old country church famed for its stained-glass windows and Lewis Carroll memorials. The author of *Alice in Wonderland* was born in the village.

The Sessions House, Daresbury: The Sessions House was built in 1841, and is now used by the pub.

Glazebury & Hitchfield Wood

START Car park opposite
Glazebury church, GR SJ673 971

DISTANCE 4 miles (6.5km)

MAPS OS Landranger
109 Manchester, Bolton &
Warrington; OS Explorer 276
Bolton, Wigan & Warrington

WHERE TO EAT AND DRINK
The Chat Moss Hotel,
Glazebury, T01925 558400

An easy walk, fairly level across fields and through woodland. Muddy in some sections after rain.

1 From the car park turn left onto the A574 and go under the railway bridge. On your left is the Chat Moss Hotel. Opposite this, take a footpath along the edge of the Manchester and Liverpool Railway. After passing through a gap, turn left at a marker post along the hedge. After ¼ mile at a way marker, turn right along a footpath which crosses a field for 100yds to a footbridge. On the other side turn right over a stile and follow the stream.

2 A further stile takes you into Hitchfield Wood. For the next ½ mile the path meanders through the wood on a permissive footpath. Access to the final section of the wood is barred, so leave by a stile on the left and turn right along the wood edge, bearing to the left to reach a signpost. Turn right here and keep straight ahead, reaching a rough track.

3 Turn right along this, under the railway, and then go straight across a field to a kissing gate. Here, follow the fence on the left and pass the earthworks on the left to a signpost; turn right across the field towards a clump of trees and follow the field edge. Pass around these on the left, and follow the marker posts right and left between fields; continuing in the same direction, make for some more, surrounding a large pond. After passing this on the left, you will reach a footbridge. Cross this and bear diagonally left across a field, following the finger-posts right and left, around a marshy area to your right. When you reach a four-way finger-post, turn right to reach another footbridge.

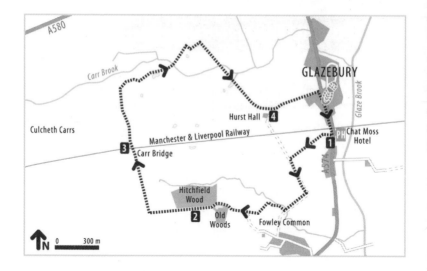

4️⃣ Cross this and keep straight ahead towards Hurst Hall. Soon the footpath becomes a rough tarmacked road, which leads past the farm access road. Turn left along this to its junction with the A574 in Glazebury. To return to the car park, turn right past All Saints church.

Points of interest

Chat Moss Hotel: This was the original booking office of Glazebury station, and the ticket window can still be seen. The name recalls Chat Moss, over which the railway crossed, the track built on bales of cotton sunk into the spongey ground!

The Manchester and Liverpool Railway: This was the first passenger railway in the world, built by George Stephenson in 1830.

Heswall Village to Parkgate

START Car park in Pye Rd by Heswall bus station, CH60 0AL, GR SJ269 818

DISTANCE 4 miles (6.5km)

MAPS OS Landranger 108 Liverpool, Southport & Wigan and OS Landranger 117 Chester & Wrexham; OS Explorer 266 Wirral & Chester

WHERE TO EAT AND DRINK Several places in Heswall and Parkgate

A fine circular walk.

From the bus station, cross Telegraph Rd (the A540) and turn left. A walk of around 100yds will bring you to Rocky La on your right. Follow the lane as it drops down to the war memorial. Turn right into Deeview Rd and immediately left down a path onto School Hill, continuing downhill to the old village. With the Black Horse Hotel on your right, cross the road and go through the gates into Heswall church, beautifully sited overlooking the River Dee. Follow the footpath that leads down through the churchyard to Rectory La. Turn left into this lane and at the end turn right into Station Rd. A short walk will bring you to Riverbank Rd and here your way is left.

[1]   As the road bears right you will see the signs for the Wirral Way on your left. Follow the Wirral Way along a well-used track, eventually passing under a bridge and then over a cart track. Continue on this track with the golf course either side until you reach a signpost and gate on the right. Walk across the golf course, staying on the marked path, towards the Dee and, on reaching the sea wall, go left along it to reach the Boat House pub.

[2]   Continue along the front, passing houses until you reach the Square on your left, where you will see an old red brick chapel. Leave the Square to the left side of the chapel and walk along School La, passing the old Schoolhouse and shortly reaching Brookland Rd. Continue ahead, passing a modern school, and, after walking under a wooden footbridge, take a footpath that leads straight ahead to the open countryside again.

[3]   Where the path ends at Wood La, turn left and follow this quiet lane to reach the busy Boathouse La. Go straight across onto a track with large metal gates and pass through these to the right-hand side. This track leads you between Backwood Farm and Backwood Hall. Where it bears to the right, go straight ahead through a marked footpath gate and into a field.

Drop down to go over a footbridge, to cross a stream. Continue straight ahead across the next field and then look ahead for a five-bar gate, to the left of which is a gate. This allows you to reach a footpath alongside the golf course; go forward with the hedge on your right.

④ Soon the path leaves the golf course and leads into a broad track flanked by big walls, which ends at the cobblestones of Gayton village, close to Gayton Hall. At the crossroads beyond Gayton Hall, turn right and proceed up Well La, a quiet avenue which, after a walk uphill of about 10mins, will bring you to Dawstone Rd. Turn left and, after walking a few yards, cross the road to reach a footpath running between houses. Turn left at the far end of this path for a short walk along Telegraph Rd, passing many shops and returning to the car park behind the bus station.

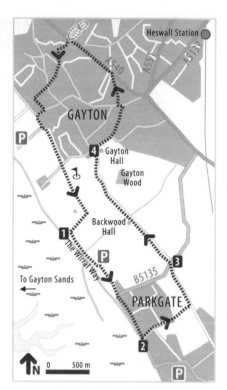

Points of interest

Parkgate: The village boasts an historic past. Phillip Sulley, writing in 1889, said: 'Parkgate in the last century was thronged with passengers to and from Ireland, from Bagilt and Flint, to which places ferry packets sailed daily, and with visitors from all parts of the country to the year 1820, when the rapid silting up of the river prevented vessels of any size from approaching the New Quay, and gradually the place waned and dropped away, and is now only a summer resort.'

Gayton Hall: This was the home of the famous Glegg family, who settled in Wirral in 1380. Like so many old houses, it has been altered and added to throughout the centuries. During the time that Parkgate was the chief port of embarkation for Ireland, it was famed for the hospitality shown to travellers. In 1689, King William III stayed the night here and, on leaving the next day, knighted his host William Glegg.

The Manchester Ship Canal

START Car park behind the Pickering Arms, WA4 2SU, GR SJ652 875

DISTANCE 4 miles (6.5km)

MAPS OS Landranger 109 Manchester, Bolton & Warrington; OS Explorer 276 Bolton, Wigan & Warrington

WHERE TO EAT AND DRINK The Pickering Arms, Thelwall, T01925 861262

An easy, fairly level walk through farmland and along canal paths.

Turn left out of the car park and take a footpath immediately on the right past the village post office. Go past the rear of several houses. The marshy area on your left here was once the course of the River Mersey, before the Manchester Ship Canal was constructed. The path reaches a stile. Do not go over this, but turn left down some steps.

① Cross two footbridges and a stile to reach the Manchester Ship Canal. Turn right up a bank above the canal. After 50yds, drop down again and follow the footpath/bridleway along the canal for 1 mile.

② This will take you under the infamous Thelwall Viaduct, which carries the M6 over the canal. The path soon becomes a wide track: follow it to its junction with another. Turn right to reach a metalled road at a sharp bend. Go right and at a T–junction turn left. After 50yds take a footpath on your right over a stile and follow a path through a small wooded area and over a disused railway. On the other side of the railway go around the front of cottages to reach the towpath of the Bridgewater Canal.

③ Keep beside the canal for 1½ miles, passing beneath the M6 again. Just before reaching the first bridge over the canal after the motorway, turn right away from the canal into a small car park. Go out onto a rough track, which crosses the disused railway again and goes down to the A56. Turn right and after 100yds take a footpath on the left, which leads through a new housing estate, emerging into a park. Go straight ahead here, passing to the right of swings to reach a rough road onto the main road through Thelwall. Turn right to return to the car park, passing the Pickering Arms on the way.

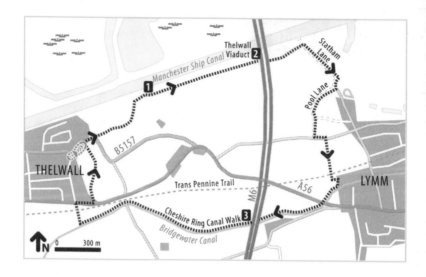

Points of interest

Manchester Ship Canal: This was built between 1887 and 1894 to allow ocean-going vessels to reach Manchester and so avoid heavy dock dues at Liverpool. It was financed by cotton mill owners and its opening made Manchester the industrial capital of Britain. The canal, which is 36 miles long and over 30ft deep, required 82 million tons of earth to be excavated.

Pickering Arms: On the wall of this pub is an inscription which reads: 'In the year 923, King Edward the Elder founded a City here and called it Thelwall'. This relates to a series of forts along the Mersey (of which Thelwall was one) that Edward built to keep out the Danes, who had conquered northern England.

START North Rode, in the lane between the school and church, SK11 0QH, GR SJ889 665

DISTANCE 4 miles (6.5km)

MAPS OS Landranger 118 Stoke-on-Trent & Macclesfield; OS Explorer 268 Wilmslow, Macclesfield & Congleton

WHERE TO EAT AND DRINK
The Plough Inn, Eaton, T01260 280207

A well-defined route offering superb views of the Dane Valley.

Follow the path straight ahead, past the church, through a gateway. At the marker post ahead turn right. Do not take the path over the cattle grid, but continue round to a stile and go over it into a field. Keeping the fence on the right, proceed to a gate and go through. Go over and turn right onto a metalled drive.

① Follow the drive through a wood and past a lovely lake to a road. Go over a railway bridge and turn right into Station Rd. At a T–junction reach the Macclesfield Canal towpath through a gap on the left beside the 'Smithy' and just before a road junction. Turn right on the towpath and go under bridge 55.

② Follow the towpath for some distance to the aqueduct taking the canal over the River Dane, where there are spectacular views along the valley. After crossing the aqueduct, leave the towpath at bridge 57 and turn right along a farm track. Follow the track down the fields, keeping a wire mesh fence on your left. Go through a gate and over a small brook, then through another gate, keeping the hedge on the left. Walk to another gate and go through to yet another gate, then across a field and under the impressive viaduct.

③ Follow the path round to the left to enter the yard of Crossley Farm. Go through the yard, past the buildings, and leave along the drive. Turn right at the road and go down to the traffic lights, taking care. Cross the bridge and take the footpath into a field on the left. Go over a grassy bank and down across a small footbridge over the river. Turn right and follow the line of the river around the field to reach a stile. Go over and straight ahead to reach a road. Turn left to return to the starting point.

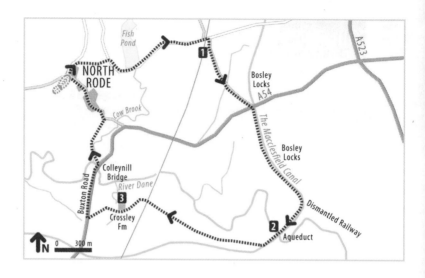

Points of interest

The Macclesfield Canal was one of the last narrow canals to be built; in fact it was very nearly a railway. It runs for 26 miles from Marple junction to Hall Green, near Kidsgrove. It is part of the 'Cheshire Ring' of canals.

START The crossroads in
Ollerton, GR SJ652 875

DISTANCE 4 miles (6.5km)

MAPS OS Landranger 118 Stoke-on-
Trent & Macclesfield; OS Explorer 268
Wilmslow, Macclesfield & Congleton

WHERE TO EAT AND DRINK
The Dun Cow, Ollerton, T01565 633093;
numerous outlets in Knutsford

A pleasant walk on the outskirts of Knutsford.

From the crossroads, follow the A537, with great care, along the pavement
towards Knutsford. Go past the Dun Cow Inn – once a courthouse – on
the right, and Ollerton Grange and Kerfield House, also on the right, to
reach a road (Manor La) on the left.

1 Do not turn along this; instead, continue for about 50yds to reach a
track, on the left, into Windmill Wood. Where the track forks, take the
right-hand branch, keeping to the edge of the woods. About 800yds from
the road the track is crossed by a path. Turn right along this, following a
superb avenue of beech and oak trees to reach a lane (Goughs La).

2 Turn right and follow the lane back to the A537. Cross, with great
care, and follow the drive of Booths Hall. Where the drive ends, walk
past Booths Hall Farm to the left side. Maintain direction along a track to
reach the end of Spring Wood, going over a stile to turn right. Go along
the north-western edge of Spring Wood, passing Springwood Farm. Go
through a gate and bear left to reach a track. Go through a farmyard and
over a stile onto a track and maintain direction ahead.

3 Turn right and follow the track through Springwood Farm. Beyond
the farm, cross four fields to reach a pond on the left. Bear right to reach a
hedge and turn right along it, following the field edge to the corner. Turn
right along the edge of Spring Wood to reach a stile, going through the
last finger of Spring Wood to reach a footbridge. Go over and turn right
through the bushes to reach the wood again. Now bear left beside a stream,
which gives the line into the next field. Follow this footpath all the way to
Ollerton Grange and bear left around the back of the house to reach the
A537 at the Dun Cow Inn. Turn left, with care, to return to Ollerton.

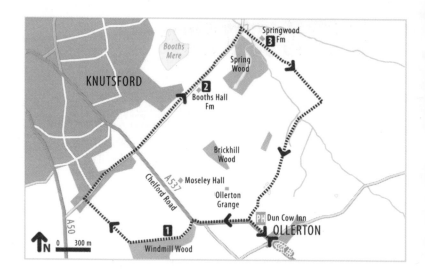

Points of interest

Knutsford: Although not on the route, many following the walk will want to visit this fine old town with its array of handsome houses. Knutsford is the 'Cranford' of Elizabeth Gaskell's novel. The author is buried in the Unitarian Chapel. The town's pride in her achievements can be gauged from the presence of a Gaskell Memorial Tower. Elizabeth was raised in a house in what is now Gaskell Avenue.

Booths Hall: The Hall is one of an elegant series of mansions close to fashionable Knutsford, the most famous being Peover Hall just a couple of miles from Ollerton. Booths Hall is Georgian and was the seat of the Legh family. It is now the headquarters of NNC, the National Nuclear Corporation, the company responsible for designing and building Britain's nuclear power stations.

Plumley & Holford Hall

START Plumley parish hall,
WA16 0TR, GR SJ717 755

DISTANCE 4 miles (6.5km)

MAPS OS Landranger 118 Stoke-on-
Trent & Macclesfield; OS Explorer
267 Northwich & Delamere Forest

WHERE TO EAT AND DRINK
The Golden Pheasant Hotel,
Plumley, T01565 722261

An easy walk, fairly level through farmland and woodland.

1   Leaving Plumley parish hall, turn right towards the station, crossing
over via the road bridge and passing The Golden Pheasant Inn. After
300yds turn right over a stile opposite Beech House Farm. Initially the
footpath skirts a plantation, then crosses a stile and follows a hedge to
your left. Cross a stile and footbridge and, after skirting a pond, keep left
beside the hedge, reaching a road through a white gate.

2   Turn right, then left into Cheadle La. After ¼ mile, take a footpath
on your right over a cattle grid. Carry on past a house, walking straight on
through a gate. Keep right at a junction, passing through a short stretch
of woodland. The track becomes much rougher; keep straight ahead. Just
before a third cattle grid, turn off to the right beside a hedge and continue
for 200yds to pass over a railway. Cross over and on the other side take a
path across the field to a gap in the trees. Turn right beside a hedge and
follow the path to its junction with a wide track. Turn left along this track
and follow to another junction.

By walking 50yds to the right, at this junction, you'll come across
an information board and viewpoint for Holford Hall; however, the
route turns left with woodlands (Plumley Lime Beds Nature Reserve) on
the right.

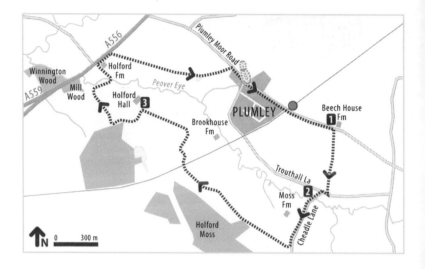

3 Continue until you reach a metal kissing gate on the right. Go through and follow a newly created path around the Holford Hall estate, going past lime beds to another gate, and turn left, going over Peover Eye and out onto the A556. Turn right here along the grass verge for 100yds and then take a footpath on your right. Follow the hedge on your left and then go straight ahead across a field to another stile. Bear left here towards a gateway with some houses beyond. Cross a stile and make for these houses, emerging onto a road, through a gate in the corner of the field. Turn right and walk back to the start.

Points of interest

Holford Hall: A beautiful black-and-white timbered house surrounded by a moat, built for Lady Mary Cholmondeley in 1601. She was famous for her lawsuits, one of which lasted 40 years. Nearby, where the bridge crosses Peover Eye, are the remains of an old watermill.

START Prestbury car
park, GR SJ902 773

DISTANCE 4 miles (6.5km)

MAPS OS Landranger 118 Stoke-on-
Trent & Macclesfield; OS Explorer 268
Wilmslow, Macclesfield & Congleton

WHERE TO EAT AND DRINK
The Bridge, T01625 829326;
Admiral Rodney, T01625 828078;
The Black Boy/The Legh, T01625
829130; The Chocolate Box, T01625
820268 (all in Prestbury)

A fine walk along the Bollin Valley.

The car park is located behind the Admiral Rodney Inn. From there, walk
north to Scott Rd and turn left. After 50yds turn right onto Bollin Way
and after about 400yds you will reach a metal kissing gate. Leaving the
tarmac track just after a playing field, continue on and at the bridge over
the River Bollin a finger-post marks the 'Bollin Valley Way'. There is a
choice now: either head north along the river bank, or turn left to cross
the bridge – whichever way you choose you will return on the other route!

1   For the book, the walk description goes left over the bridge and along
to a stile beside a cattle grid. Proceed 200yds up the drive to a gateway at
Spittle House, then west over a stile on the left, bearing right along the
edge of two pasture fields to a good wooden kissing gate. After 50yds drop
down to a wooden bridge over a brook and follow a well-trodden path
between fences for 400yds, coming out at the gateway of Lower Gadhole
farm. Turn left at the gate and travel along a gravel track to the tarmac
Greendale La. At the gateway of Woodend Farm House go over a stile
on the right into a field. Walk over and bypass a stile beside a metal gate,
going straight on.

2   After 50yds go over a stile and at the next metal kissing gate walk
between laurel hedges to a circular tarmac area at Legh Old Hall. After
50yds turn right between Legh Old Hall and Legh Hall onto a cobbled
slabbed drive. After 50yds go through a metal kissing gate, then proceed
and go over a stile next to a metal gate and past stables at Woodside Farm.
Walk 50yds to a wooden kissing gate and turn left onto a track beside a
golf course. Ignore the finger-post pointing north and walk bearing left
past an old brick barn with quirky brickwork.

③ After 100yds go through a gap in the fence into woodland and after 100yds emerge back onto the golf course. Follow the mowed path for 50yds to a short marker post and bear left across the course to a single pine tree by tee no.13. Go over to the trees ahead and to a stile and down to a long wooden bridge over the River Bollin. At the finger-post on the other side follow the Bollin Way marker right beside the river. Follow the river path past sewage works, until you reach a black metal kissing gate and back to the start.

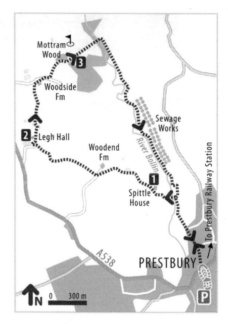

Points of interest

The beautiful village of Prestbury has a long history, as the name – from the Saxon for Priest's Town – and a Saxon, or even, perhaps, Danish, cross in the churchyard attest. The idea of the town having been founded by a roving evangelical priest also lives on in Priest La and the Priest's House, a superb fifteenth-century building. St Peter's church is Norman in origin, but from that period only the magnificent doorway remains. The ancient cross is housed in a glass case in the churchyard. In a tradition that dates back to the sixteenth century, the church bell rings a curfew at 8 o'clock each evening, the number of strikes corresponding to the date in the month.

Rode Mill & Little Moreton Hall

START The church, Rode Mill, GR SJ824 575

DISTANCE 4 miles (6.5km)

MAPS OS Landranger 118 Stoke-on-Trent & Macclesfield; OS Explorer 268 Wilmslow, Macclesfield & Congleton

WHERE TO EAT AND DRINK
Little Moreton Hall (tea room inside house); The Rising Sun Inn, Station Rd, Scholar Green, To1782 776235

A short, well-marked walk on the urban fringe, with fine architectural and historical interest.

Walk east down the lane at the side of the church and after 150yds go right over a stile before a stream. Follow a track, keeping to the right of a row of trees, and walk to a stile by two metal gates. Go over and left across a stream. Go up a lane to the main road and cross, going left up Station Rd. Follow this for 600yds to a three-storey farm.

1 Turn left at a sign for Low Farm, but if you wish to go to The Rising Sun Inn, carry on 150yds along Station Rd. Follow a tarmac lane for 500yds towards Low Farm, reaching a stile on the right beside a wood. There are good views of Mow Cop Folly to the right here.

2 On reaching the canal, turn left along the towpath for 600yds to a bridge. Ramsdell Hall is the fine and rambling property on the opposite bank here. Go left at the bridge, through two metal kissing gates and continue in a more or less straight line, over stiles. The eerie Great Moreton Hall appears out of woodland to your right. When you cross a stile by a gate, turn left to the magnificent Little Moreton Hall and follow signposts for the South Cheshire Way.

3 At the road entrance to Little Moreton Hall and main road, go left for 100yds then right at a footpath sign in the hedge. Continue over stiles and keep following the marked footpath signs. When you reach Boarded Barn Farm, turn right at a track with a marker post.

4 Follow the path to Moors Farm and then a track to the lane at Rode Mill House. Turn left back to the start.

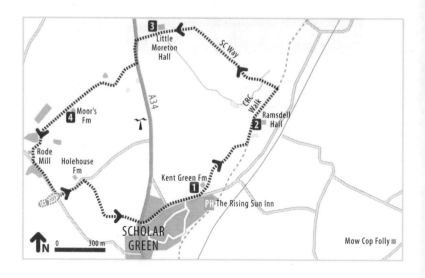

Points of interest

Mow Cop Folly: At 1,090ft (333m) above sea level, Mow Cop offers extensive views across the Cheshire Plain and beyond. It was built in ruinous style by Randle Wilbraham in 1750 and is associated with the early days of the revival of non-conformism and the establishment of Primitive Methodism.

Little Moreton Hall: Begun in the fifteenth century, it is one of Britain's finest examples of a timber-framed, moated manor house. There are superb carved gables and recently discovered and restored sixteenth-century wall paintings.

START Hadlow Road station,
Willaston, GR SJ331 773

DISTANCE 4 miles (6.5km)

MAPS OS Landranger 117
Chester & Wrexham; OS Explorer
266 Wirral & Chester

WHERE TO EAT AND DRINK The
Pollard Inn, Willaston, 0151 327 4615

An easy walk, fairly level, through farmland and along a disused railway
converted into a country park.

Adjacent to the car park is the restored Hadlow Road station. At the far
end of the platform, a gate leads out onto Hadlow Rd. Cross this and go
through the gateway opposite. The old railway beyond is now the Wirral
Way, a long-distance footpath and part of the Wirral Country Park. Follow
the Way for about 300yds, turning right through a metal kissing gate, and
follow a marked path ahead until it reaches a cul-de-sac. Walk through
to emerge into the car park of the Pollard Inn, where refreshments may
be obtained.

Go through the car park, but just before the road, take a footpath between
the car park and some houses, which leads into the centre of Willaston
with its attractive green. Go past the green and turn left along the B5133.
Shortly you will see a church on your right. Turn along a footpath by the
side of this. After passing some garages, turn left around the back of the
church and then right into a housing estate. Just before the first house, a
footpath runs left around the backs of several houses and then out into
a sports field. Turn right in the field, keeping the hedge on the right and
following it through several metal kissing gates to a metalled road.

1 Turn right. On your left you will see The Old Mill. Just beyond the
mill take a bridleway on your left beside Mill House with a signpost for
'Raby'. Go along this for 200yds and then take a footpath on your right
through a metal kissing gate. Cross a stile and follow a hedge for ½ mile
– this hedge is the Cheshire county boundary. Continue until you reach a
rough bridleway; turn right and follow the bridleway, which, after about
400yds, becomes a metalled lane that leads to the B5133. Cross into Heath
La opposite and follow this for about 600yds.

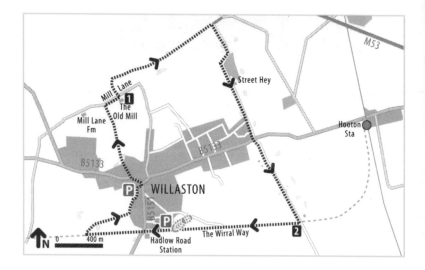

2   Just before the road climbs to cross the Wirral Way, take a footpath on your right. At the bottom of a slope, turn right, back onto the Wirral Way, and follow it back to the car park and start.

Points of interest

Hadlow Road station: This has been restored and refurbished to appear just as it would have done on a typical day in 1952, the year the line closed down. Everything has been re-created down to the last detail.

Willaston: Although it is today mostly a modern village, the centre of Willaston is very old, with a number of fascinating buildings, dating from the sixteenth and seventeenth centuries, grouped around an attractive village green. Most of these buildings are old farms, the formation now being unique in the Wirral.

The Old Mill: Built in 1800, this was the largest of the old Wirral flour mills. At the top it had five sets of grinding stones, driven by wind and used for grinding cattle food, while on the ground floor there were four sets of bigger grinding stones, driven by steam, for making wheat into flour. In 1930 a storm broke its sails and it was forced to close. Today it is a rather unusual private house.

Alsager & the Merelake Way

START Car park at the start of the
Merelake Way, GR SJ807 550

DISTANCE 4½ miles (7km)

MAPS OS Landranger 118 Stoke-on-
Trent & Macclesfield; OS Explorer 268
Wilmslow, Macclesfield & Congleton

WHERE TO EAT AND DRINK
The Linley Tavern, Talke Rd,
Alsager, T01270 882732

A pleasant, easy walk with a wide variety of flowers and wildlife.

①   From the car park, walk south along the full length of the line, now
the Merelake Way, but take the opportunity to climb some of the steps at
the side to enjoy the views. At the end of the line turn right onto Merelake
Rd, then left at the T–junction with the main road. Go to the left-hand
bend with chevron markings and take the footpath signposted to the
right. Follow the brook to a footbridge, cross and go ahead with the hedge
on your right and pass a pylon to a gate next to the third telegraph pole.
Go over and continue in the same direction with the hedge on your left.
Cross four more stiles and after the fourth turn right with the hedge on
your right to reach a gap in the corner of the field.

②   Follow the hedge on the right to a double stile and turn left. As a
farm comes into view, cross a stile on the left and go past the farm, bearing
right to reach a track. Follow the track down to Station Rd. Turn left, then
right into Talke Rd to return to the car park.

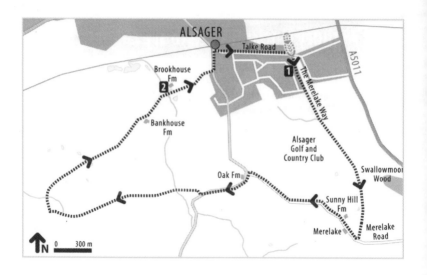

Points of interest

The Merelake Way is a disused railway line – one of a number in Cheshire that have been developed for walking and wildlife preservation. It was formerly known as the Audley Branch Line and was used mainly for carrying coal from the mines in Stoke-on-Trent, although some passenger trains did run. The line closed in 1963 owing to the decline in the mining industry in the area.

44 Astbury (including Astbury Lake)

START Egerton Arms, Astbury, CW12
4RQ, GR SJ845 615 (park in pub car
park if intending to visit, or there's a
small parking area by the entrance
to the churchyard opposite the pub)

DISTANCE 4½ miles (7km)

MAPS OS Explorer 268 Wilmslow,
Macclesfield & Congleton

WHERE TO EAT AND DRINK
Egerton Arms, Astbury, 01260
273946 (opposite the church)

A gentle and easy circular walk, taking in local paths and tracks including part of
Astbury golf course, Macclesfield Canal and Astbury Lake.

Facing the entrance to the Egerton Arms with St Mary's church opposite,
go east along Peel La and shortly turn into School La. On reaching a large
house ahead, in about 200yds and at the fork in the lane, go right and
then after a further 200yds turn right into a field through a kissing gate.
Follow the clearly marked path (hedge to right), and continue across
the field through another kissing gate (hedge now on left). Keep on
this path until you reach a wooded area with a stream running through
it. Cross the footbridge and continue onto the golf course. Cross over
the fairway, passing the putting green to the left, and continue towards
another wooded area where there is a clear opening. Look for the yellow
waymark ahead. Follow the path through the wood and emerge onto the
Macclesfield Canal by a footbridge.

1️⃣ Turn left and walk along the canal for about 600yds, reaching a
bridge. Just before the bridge turn left through an opening and up steps
onto Lambert's La. Turn left (signed Fol Hollow) and continue for about
880yds. Go through a gate and continue along the track as it descends
until you reach a fork in the path. Take the right arm and cross the
footbridge. Continue along the track until a junction is reached. Turn
sharp right onto Stony La, which leads to a main road (500yds).

2️⃣ Turn left and in about 75yds turn right into Banky Fields. Keeping to
the right, go up the road and over a grassy area and turn right onto a path,
with steps, downhill. At the bottom turn left and down more steps to the
lake's edge. Turn right and proceed around the edge of Astbury Lake.

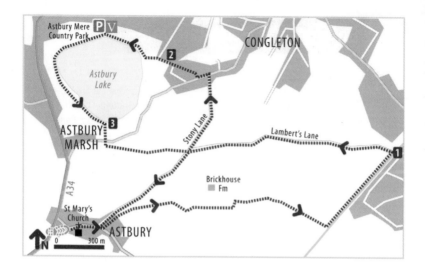

③ Continue round until a boatyard is reached in about ¾ mile. Just beyond the boatyard is a small parking area and at its furthest edge turn right and up onto a path and into trees. Follow the path to a road (Fol Hollow) and cross over to a track opposite. Follow the track (500yds), arriving at the junction of Lambert's La and Stony La.

Turn right at the end of the disused farm onto a path signed Astbury. Follow the path across three smallish fields and down a short track into School La. Follow this back to the start point via Peel La.

Points of interest

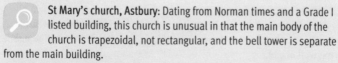 **St Mary's church, Astbury:** Dating from Norman times and a Grade I listed building, this church is unusual in that the main body of the church is trapezoidal, not rectangular, and the bell tower is separate from the main building.

Astbury Lake: This used to be a sand quarry; now it is noted for its bird population and sail boarding.

Bollington & Berristall Dale

START Car park in Bollington, opposite the Spinners Arms, SK10 5PW, GR SJ937 779

DISTANCE 4½ miles (7km)

MAPS OS Landranger 118 Stoke-on-Trent & Macclesfield; OS Explorer 268 Wilmslow, Macclesfield & Congleton

WHERE TO EAT AND DRINK Plenty of pubs in Bollington

A walk through hilly terrain with some splendid views. Wellingtons or boots advised.

Leave the car park by the main entrance and turn left at the main road. Continue uphill and turn right into Church St, passing St John's church on your right. At a T–junction turn left, passing houses along a road.

①   Walk up the lane, passing the site of Ingersley Mill to the finger-post on the left – this is the Gritstone Trail. Cross the bridge in the field and then follow an obvious track uphill and to the left (once a path used by mill workers walking into Bollington). Squeeze through a stone gap and go forward with a wall on your left. Big Low will come into view directly ahead, and you continue straight on over fields and through kissing gates. Ignore a Gritstone Trail marker when it indicates a sharp left, and continue to reach a wide gateway. Turn right here onto a farm track, which you follow uphill for approximately ¼ mile. 50yds before the top of the rise, turn left through a gate, crossing the field with the fence on your left to reach a well-defined track. Follow the track through the farmyard to join a minor road, and turn left to stay on this track to a T–junction.

Stay right at the T–junction to walk down to a main road, turning left and then immediately right at a waymark sign. Take the right-hand of two tracks – downhill – and follow this for 500yds. Just past a stone building on the left cross a gate, also on the left, and go to the right, continuing downhill to cross a stile to the right of a large holly bush. Keep the hedge and fence on your right, until where they bend to the right, keep straight ahead and cross a stile. Cut through the yard to a gate on the right, and follow the track downhill to two footbridges, and then bear uphill to a stile in the wall ahead.

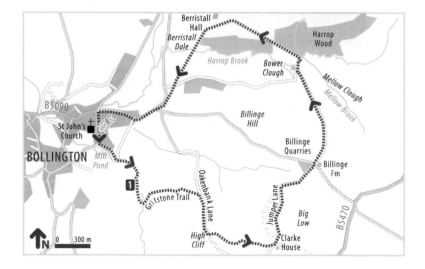

Carry on the track ahead, gently rising uphill, until you go over the third cattle grid. You will see a marker post beside the track, where you bear left downhill to a telegraph pole and pass between ponds. Go through a gate by the marker post, turn left and continue down a distinct path. Pass through a gate and over a small packhorse bridge, then bear left uphill to the top and follow the track through fields and gates to a minor road. Turn right here to join a road, and then left to follow the road to a junction. Turn right here at the signpost for Bollington and walk back into the town and the car park on the B5090.

Points of interest

St John's church: Consecrated in 1834 by the Bishop of Chester. The churchyard has 10 war graves, all of which are maintained by the War Graves Commission.

Bollington: A former mill town, with many stone houses. There was also extensive quarrying around Bollington of Kerridge free stone, valued for its whiteness. From it the nave of Christ Church, Oxford, and also the promenade gardens of Douglas on the Isle of Man are made.

Chester Meadows

START Bridgegate, Chester,
GR SJ406 658

DISTANCE 4½ miles (7km)

MAPS OS Landranger 117
Chester & Wrexham; OS Explorer
266 Wirral & Chester

WHERE TO EAT AND DRINK There
are numerous places in Chester

The old city and delightful water meadows.

From Bridgegate cross the Old Dee Bridge and turn left along the path
that follows the Dee's bank. Go under the suspension bridge, built in 1852
as a footbridge for city folk to reach the new Queen's Park. The Park itself
lies to the right a little way further on.

① The path now follows a gentle curve of the river. In this section the
water meadows are known as the Earl's Eye. As the meadows were flooded
by each high tide the name presumably derives from the fact that it, too,
watered occasionally!

Continue along the river, passing on the opposite bank the moorings
of Chester Sailing Club. Ahead now is a gate. Go through, continuing
along the bank top path through the water meadows along a good flat
path. Keep along the river bank to reach a metal kissing gate close to a
stone marked CNR 1972 (erected to commemorate the beating of the
bounds in 1972 by the Mayor of Chester, C. N. Ribbeck).

② Go through the gate and turn right along the boundary hedge of a
house called Heronbridge to reach a kissing gate onto a road (Eaton Rd,
which follows the old Roman road).

Turn right and walk to Greenbank, a fine early nineteenth-century
house. Opposite this is a gate, and to the left of this a path heads into
woodland. Take this, bearing left at first, then continuing through the
woodland to reach a crossing drive.

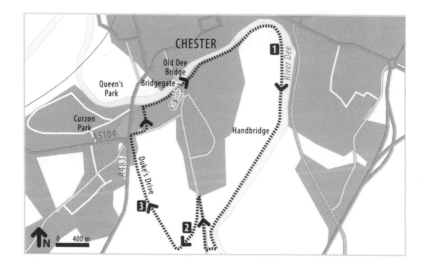

③   Turn right along the drive, Duke's Drive, following it to the fine wrought-iron gates where it reaches the A483. Turn right along this road, soon going into Overleigh Rd. Now cross the road and turn left into River La. Where the road goes sharply right to run parallel with the river, go with it, bearing left to follow the riverbank back to the Old Dee Bridge. There, turn left to return to Bridgegate.

Points of interest

Bridgegate: This was one of the few main gates through the Chester town walls, guarding the Dee crossing and the shortest route to Wales.

Old Dee Bridge: This massive old bridge was built thick and squat to survive the occasional battering from the Dee. At this point the Dee is tidal and numerous bridges had been washed away before this stone bridge was erected around 1400.

Queen's Park: This piece of land was given to the city by the Duke of Westminster in 1867 and was laid out for the benefit of the city folk soon after. The name commemorates Queen Victoria. The grateful Chester citizens raised a statue to the Duke in 1869.

Duke's Drive: The name derives from this having been one of the drives to the Duke of Westminister's mansion, Eaton Hall, at Eccleston to the south.

Culcheth & Croft

START Car park at Culcheth Linear Park, GR SJ649 949

DISTANCE 4½ miles (7km)

MAPS OS Landranger 109 Manchester, Bolton & Warrington; OS Explorer 276 Bolton, Wigan & Warrington

WHERE TO EAT AND DRINK The General Elliot Hotel, Croft, T01925 766900

An easy, fairly level walk through farmland and along a disused railway.

From the car park, walk towards the railway bridge, and go up some steps to Wigshaw La. Turn right along this and after 100yds go left into Glaziers La. Just beyond Glaziers Lane Farm take a footpath on the right through a gap in the hedge and follow the hedge on your left. Continue heading along the path, passing fish ponds and a stile, to walk across fields until reaching a marker post. Turn right here and walk across the field to a stile and keep straight ahead across several fields to reach Lady La. Turn left into the lane and after 50yds take a footpath on your right. Cross the field to a stile and then continue straight ahead towards a clump of trees in the middle of the next field. Here, bear slightly left to reach a gap in the hedge opposite. A path beyond leads between high hedges and emerges at Abbey Close.

1 Turn right here to the main road, and turn right again along the road, and soon you will reach a road junction, beside which is The General Elliot, where refreshments may be obtained at the halfway point. Take the left fork past the pub and, after 100yds, take a footpath on the left. Beyond Mount Pleasant House the track disappears, so keep straight ahead across the fields to a marker post. Turn right here along an old field boundary, marked by a line of solitary oaks. Continue on this path, following the marker posts and a field boundary to reach Stone Pit La.

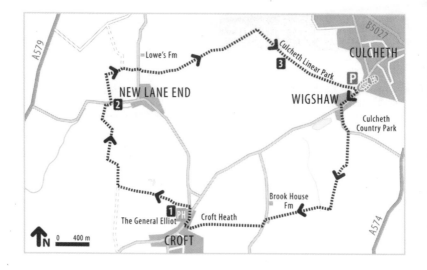

② Turn right along this into the hamlet of New Lane End. Turn left at the Plough Inn and, after 200yds, take a footpath on your right. This runs beside a ditch at first, but then crosses the ditch into an open field, towards a clump of trees, where you will meet a rough track. Follow this around the trees to a path junction. Go directly across this, walking under a telegraph line. After passing through a gap in the hedge, walk straight across the field to a gap opposite.

③ There, a flight of steps drops down into Culcheth Linear Park. Turn right now along the bed of an old railway track. This is pleasantly wooded and is an attractive end to the walk as you cover the last mile back to the car park.

Points of interest

Culcheth Linear Park: This was originally the Wigan to Glazebrook railway, constructed in 1878 to aid the commercial extraction of peat from Risley Moss. The line closed down in 1965 and was then converted into the lovely country park which exists today.

Gawsworth Hall

START Gawsworth Hall,
SK11 9RN, GR SJ892 694

DISTANCE 4½ miles (7km)

MAPS OS Landranger 118 Stoke-on-Trent & Macclesfield; OS Explorer 268 Wilmslow, Macclesfield & Congleton

WHERE TO EAT AND DRINK
Nowhere on the route

In search of Shakespeare's 'Dark Lady'.

Walk eastwards between Gawsworth Hall and the ponds to the north of it. Just beyond the last pond there is a gate; go through it and walk along the field edge on the right to reach another gate. Cross several more fields, all linked by kissing gates to reach a road.

1 Turn right, soon passing Mount Farm. Ignore a turning to the right, going over a railway bridge and passing Whereton Farm, to the right, and Fodens Farm, to the left. Further along, a shortcut can be made to the Macclesfield Canal (see note to Walks 8 & 9) by going up the track to Woodhouse End and crossing the fields beyond, but you may also continue along the lane for ½ mile to reach the canal towpath.

2 Turn left along the towpath, following it for about 1 mile to reach bridge 47. Now go along a path on the left and cross the railway line via a bridge to reach a path into Danes Moss Nature Reserve.

3 Go under power lines and between two copses to reach a crossroads of paths. Go straight over to reach a stile. Go over this and follow the right-hand field boundary to a corner by a house. Turn left here, exiting the field onto a road. Turn right along the road to reach a T–junction. Now turn left on a signed path across several fields to reach a road. Turn left and follow the road back to Gawsworth Hall.

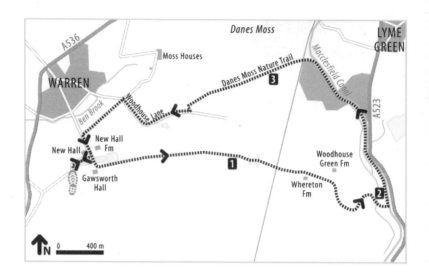

Points of interest

Gawsworth Hall is a privately owned, half-timbered Tudor mansion open to the public, beautifully set in parkland with large ponds. Inside, some of the rooms are original sixteenth century, and there is a fine art collection including works by Constable and Turner. At the back of the house is one of the few (and arguably the best) remaining examples of a medieval tilting ground, some 200 x 60yds. Here, tournaments were held in the late sixteenth century. The Hall was home to Samuel 'Maggoty' Johnson, England's last professional jester, who died in 1773. At his request, he was buried in Maggoty Johnson's Wood a little way to the north. The Hall was also the home of Mary Fitton, maid of honour at Elizabeth I's court and claimed by many to be the 'Dark Lady' of Shakespeare's sonnets.

Redesmere

START Car park at the southern tip of Redesmere, GR SJ848 713

DISTANCE 4½ miles (7km) or 7½ miles (12km)

MAPS OS Landranger 118 Stoke-on-

Trent & Macclesfield; OS Explorer 268 Wilmslow, Macclesfield & Congleton

WHERE TO EAT AND DRINK Nowhere on the route but refreshments are available at nearby Morton and Withington

A fine lake and a mysterious hall.

The car park alongside Redesmere is reached by turning off the A34 towards Fanshawe. Return to the road.

The shorter route leaves here, going over a stile onto a signed path, heading south-east across fields. After crossing several fields, Simonswood Farm comes into view. Head towards this to reach a road (the B5392).

① Turn right along the road, passing Siddington church to the left, to reach the A34. Turn right and follow the main road to Redesmere Farm, to the right. Here, cross the road to reach a track by thatched cottages and follow it westward. Go to the left of another thatched cottage, then round a hut to reach Snape Brook and the longer route.

The longer route continues along the road towards Fanshawe. Go past Hills Green Farm, on the right; then, where a lane joins from the left, go over a stile on the right, close to Fanshawe Brook. Cross several fields, linked by stiles, aiming for Hazelwall Farm. The stiles point you to the right of the farm, the final one taking you onto the drive. Turn right and walk down to the B5392. Cross and follow Henshaw La opposite, to reach a fork. Take the right-hand branch, a track, and follow it to Henshaw Hall Farm. Go through the farm, continuing along the track to go through Herskey Wood.

② Continue to the edge of the next wood (Moss Wood), bearing left along its eastern edge, and then left to reach Crabtree Moss Farm. Go through the farm and follow its drive to a road. Turn right, but after about 350 yards, just after passing a house on the left, turn right along a track, following it to a stile. Go over and turn right to continue along the track. It goes past a wood, to the left, then on through the large Northwood Farm.

③ Stay with the track to go through Sandbank Farm and on to reach the A34. Turn left for 200yds, then cross, with great care, and turn right

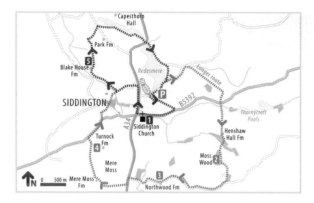

along Blackden La. Follow the road past a wood (Mere Moss) to the right, continuing to reach a farm drive, also on the right. Go along the drive, through the farm, and cross several fields linked by stiles to reach a crossing drive. To the right here is Turnock Farm. However, the route turns left, following the drive to the B5392.

4 Turn right and follow the road to Dickery Cottage, to the left. Turn left along a path just beyond, following it to its junction with another path by a pair of gates. Here, turn very sharply right, but after a few yards go left along another path. Follow this path to a road. Turn right, then first left. Now maintain direction on a path that goes through woodland to reach a stream. Cross and walk forward to reach a crossing track. Turn left, rejoining the shorter route.

5 Follow the track to reach the drive to Blake House Farm. Turn right along the drive, going through the farm and continuing on a track to reach the next stile. Cross several fields and stiles, bearing left of Park Farm, until you reach a lane. Opposite is a bungalow; walk through a gate beside it and along a track towards Capesthorne Hall, but bear right and walk alongside the lakes, continuing along the edge of a wood to reach the A34. Cross with great care, going onto a path in the trees opposite, and follow the path beyond along the shore of Redesmere, ignoring the tempatation to turn left along a lane to Fanshawe, to reach the minor road used to start the walk. Turn right to reach the start.

Points of interest

Capesthorne Hall: This superb Jacobean Hall is said to be haunted by a severed hand that scratches at the windows.

Redesmere: The delightfully set lake is a haven for birdlife.

START Tegg's Nose Country Park visitors' centre, SK11 0AP, GR SJ950 733

DISTANCE 4½ miles (7km)

MAPS OS OL24 The Peak District

WHERE TO EAT AND DRINK
Leather's Smithy, T01260 252313 (near Ridgegate Reservoir; busy particularly at weekends but well worth the wait)

A challenging walk with a difficult descent but spectacular views of the area.

Exit the Country Park by the visitors' centre and turn left along a path for about 450yds for a further left turn onto the Gritstone Trail.

① Follow the track for about 650yds, passing a small exhibition of stone-working machinery on the way.

② At this point there is a footpath to the right to Tegg's Nose summit, rejoining the track just before a left turn with a fine viewpoint across the valley and with Shutlingsloe in the distance.

Follow the Gritstone trail downwards to an exit into a small car park. Here, the trail crosses the dams of Tegg's Nose and Bottoms Reservoirs. Turn left by Bottoms Reservoir and join Clarke La in about 100yds. Follow the lane eastwards for about 700yds to a fork in the lane by the Leather's Smithy Inn (care must be taken along here as the pavement is very narrow).

③ Take the left fork and in about 700yds take a further left onto a woodland road. Continue up the forest road for about 1,200yds to a clearing in the forest.

④ Turn left past the ruined building, keeping to the right, and continue for about 200yds then turn right onto a footpath. In about 100yds the path joins Hacked Way La. Turn left and immediately right onto a footpath, going across a field and past a house (Ashtreetop). The path continues over three fields to Warrilowhead Farm.

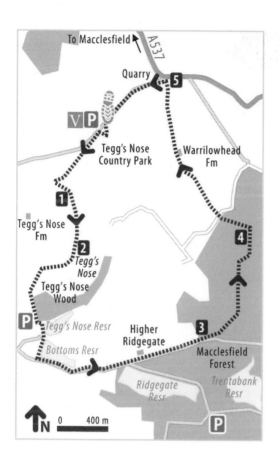

⑤ Pass to the left of the farm and after three further fields turn right onto a lane and in less than 100yds turn left onto a footpath. On reaching the Buxton Old Rd, turn left for about 900yds then right into the Country Park (care should be taken on this leg of the walk as there are no footpaths on the road).

Points of interest

Tegg's Nose Country Park: There is a visitors' centre, providing information about the area.

START Car park in Timbersbrook, GR SJ895 628

DISTANCE 5 miles (8km)

MAPS OS Landranger 118 Stoke-on-Trent & Macclesfield; OS Explorer 268 Wilmslow, Macclesfield & Congleton

WHERE TO EAT AND DRINK
Coach & Horses Inn, near Timbersbrook, T01260 273019

A fine walk to an excellent viewpoint.

From the car park go back to the road (Weathercock La) and turn right. The road descends to cross Timbers Brook, from which the village takes its name. Ignore the first turning to the right, but take the second (Acorn La). Though called a lane, it's more of a rough track. Follow to a road and cross into another rough lane, Gosberryhole La. This rises steeply around a sharp left-hand bend, then more gently past Folly Cottage. Nearing the top, the lane approaches the National Trust woodland of Bosley Cloud. Bear left, where the path indicates three routes, to walk along the woodland's western edge. The view from this section of the walk makes the effort of arriving here worthwhile.

① Follow the woodland edges as it bears right to reach the trig point summit of Bosley Cloud. From the summit the path continues eastwards, then descends steep steps to reach a track. Turn right along this, but where it bears sharply away from the woodland edge, go over a stile and follow the path along the edge to a path junction. Turn left here to reach a path fork. Now take the left-hand branch, following the path back to Gosberryhole La. Turn left along the lane, following it to reach a road.

② Turn left to visit the Bridestones. Having visited the stones, go back along the road, following it to a crossroads. Go straight over here and at the next crossroads, to reach the Coach and Horses Inn at a Y–junction.

③ Turn right to the inn, the walk continuing by following the road past a junction and back into Timbersbrook. At the crossroads in the centre of the village, turn left into Weathercock La to return to the starting car park.

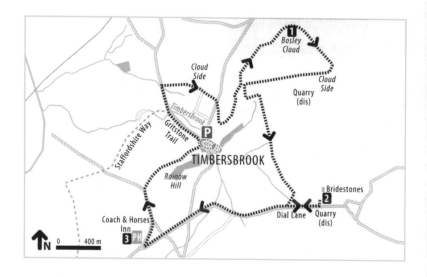

Points of interest

 View: The view from this point of the walk is dominated by the Jodrell Bank radio telescope, the 250ft diameter hemisphere to the north-west. Closer to hand is the town of Congleton, once a silk-making centre.

Bosley Cloud: Despite its lowly altitude – just 1,125ft (343m) – the Cloud stands high above the east Cheshire plain, making it an exceptional viewpoint, particularly of the western edge of the Peak District National Park. The summit sits on the border between Cheshire and Staffordshire, and though referred to only as 'The Cloud' on OS maps, it is more properly named after the Staffordshire village on the hill's north-eastern base, beside Bosley Reservoir.

Bridestones: The stones are the remains of a Neolithic burial chamber. The long barrow that once covered the huge stone slabs is believed to have been 300ft long. The burial chamber itself was 18ft long.

START The Bear's Head, Brereton Green, CW11 1RS, GR SJ775 644

DISTANCE 5 miles (8km)

MAPS OS Landranger 118 Stoke-on-Trent & Macclesfield; OS Explorer 268 Wilmslow, Macclesfield & Congleton

WHERE TO EAT AND DRINK
The Bear's Head, Brereton Green, T01477 544732

A very pleasant walk on level ground with plenty to see.

From the Bear's Head turn left past Smithy Cottage and pass under an archway joining twin lodges and inscribed Brereton Hall School.

① Go straight up the driveway, which bears right past the school and the adjoining church of St Oswald's. Go past the church and fork right onto a hardcore path. Go through two gates onto a long, well-made track. Follow the track all the way past a farm, where it turns left, until you reach the end at a T–junction.

② Cross straight over and enter Brereton Heath Park at the signed footpath. Follow the footpath straight ahead, avoiding the many side turnings to arrive at the mere. There is a good surfaced path around the mere. Turn right, following it for 100yds, and at the sign for Brimstone Trail bear right, following the yellow marker posts through the trees to a metal kissing gate that leads onto a bridleway. Turn right, keeping the fence on your right, and proceed down the bridleway back to the road. Go across and over a stile to join a footpath into a field. Keep the wire mesh fence on your left and cross a stile marked 'only use footpath if you know the route'. Go straight ahead and cross a bridge over a small brook.

③ Continue straight across two fields and stiles to where Smethwick Hall Farm comes into view. Cross the last field, aiming for the left of the row of trees lining the drive, and leave via a stile to emerge on a bend of the road. Turn right and right again into a drive leading to Smethwick Hall Barns. Turn left over a stile just before the buildings.

Go straight ahead with hawthorns on your left to reach a line of telegraph poles. Follow the poles to a footbridge and stile. Go over and keep the hedgrow on your right. Leave the field over a stile. Turn right on the road, which leads back to Brereton Green and the car.

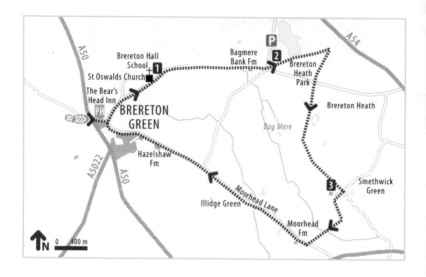

Points of interest

Brereton Hall: A splendid building completed around 1600 on the site of an earlier hall. It was modelled on a hall at Rock Savage near Clifton Runcorn where Sir William Brereton, an orphan, was raised. The Brereton family lived here until 1722 when the male line died out. It was taken over as a private school during World War II. It is now privately owned and is not open to the public.

St Oswald's church: The original church dates back to the time of Richard I but the present building only to 1600. Sadly the church is kept locked but a wander round the grounds is rewarding and the key can be obtained from the rectory.

Brereton Heath Park: Formerly a sand quarry, the area is now a country park. The mere is home to a wide variety of birds as well as a sailing club.

START At the roadside next to the Chapel House Inn, Burtonwood, WA5 4PT, GR SJ565 929

DISTANCE 5 miles (8km)

MAPS OS Landranger 108 Liverpool, Southport & Wigan; OS Explorer 276 Bolton, Wigan & Warrington

WHERE TO EAT AND DRINK
The Chapel House Inn, Burtonwood, T01925 225607; The Fiddle i'th Bag, Burtonwood, T01925 225442

An easy, fairly level walk across fields and along a canal towpath.

From the car park turn left past the pub and the church. On the right you will see the parish hall and beside this a footpath leading right between houses. Follow this to open countryside. Keep ahead beside a hedge and then a fence to where the footpath meets a broad track. Turn left and then immediately right, crossing a large field through two gates, to a broken stile beside some solitary trees. On its far side, cross a field to a metalled road through a pinch gap. Turn right to reach the Warrington–Burtonwood road. Go left up to the roundabout and left to a farm track.

Follow the farm access road and pass through the farmyard on its left. Follow the hedge for ½ mile, keeping to the left through this, and swinging around to the right alongside a fence. Keep along the field path with a ditch on your left until you reach a finger-post. Follow the path to a second finger-post and cross the field diagonally right to another finger-post. Turn left before reaching the pylon; the path crosses a large field divided by Phipps Brook, over which is a footbridge. On the other side cross the field to a marker post and turn right onto a broad track and follow this to a metalled road.

1 Turn left along this, to its junction with Alder La. Opposite is the Fiddle i'th Bag Inn, where refreshments are available. Turn left and then immediately right down Hall La. After 400yds take a footpath right, go over a footbridge crossing Sankey Brook and then diagonally left across a field on a well-defined route to reach a towpath of a restored section of the St Helens Canal.

Bear left along the towpath and follow it for over 1 mile through the attractive parkland of the Sankey Valley Linear Park. When you reach the first bridge over the canal at the Mucky Mountains site, turn left across a footbridge back over Sankey Brook and then bear right uphill.

2 At the top of a short climb turn left along a broad footpath. Soon you will pass the access road leading to Bradlegh Old Hall. Carry straight on past the access road to reach a metalled road. Turn right along this to a T–junction, on the edge of Burtonwood. Opposite is a footpath skirting the edge of a housing estate. Take this and follow it along a path between fences to emerge onto the main village road near the church. Turn right and return to the car park.

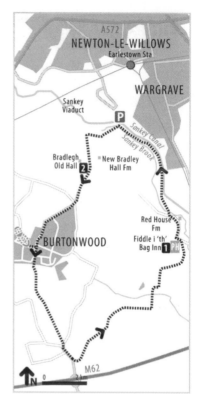

Points of interest

Burtonwood Airfield: Formerly an RAF base, it was taken over in 1942 by the Americans, who used it as a maintenance and repair unit. A huge warehouse built in 1956 is one of the largest covered storage depots in Europe.

St Helens Canal: Opened in 1757, this was the first stillwater navigation in England. It was constructed to carry coal from St Helens to Liverpool and stimulated the growth of the chemical industry in Widnes.

Bradlegh Old Hall: Surrounding the nineteenth-century farmhouse are the remains of Sir Peter Legh's fortified manor house built in 1465. The gatehouse, with its tiny chapel, and the moat survive today. In the farmhouse is an old bed in which Richard III is reputed to have slept.

Mucky Mountains: The Mucky Mountains in Earlestown are by-products of the chemical industry – in this case soda-making – in the 1830s.

55 Great Barrow

START Great Barrow
church, GR SJ469 684

DISTANCE 5 miles (8km)

MAPS OS Landranger 117
Chester & Wrexham; OS Explorer
266 Wirral & Chester

WHERE TO EAT AND DRINK
A general store in Great Barrow
serves hot and cold refreshments

A quiet exploration of the Cheshire Plain.

Go down to the B5132, which curves its way through Great Barrow's
western edge, and turn right along it to the crossroads.

1 Turn left into Ferma La and after 150yds turn right (this is the first
turning right) and follow a track up Barrow Hill, reaching a house at the
top. Here, go left over a stile. From this point the view looks across the
Cheshire Plain, as well as Stanlow and Ellesmere Port to the north. Cross
a field to a stile, go over and follow the edge of the field beyond downhill
to reach another stile. Go over onto a track and turn right along it. Turn
right, off the track, at a signed path, climbing uphill to reach a gateway. Go
through and bear left along a hedge to reach some steps. Descend these to
reach a lane and turn right along it to reach the B5132. The Old Foxcote
Inn is diagonally opposite, although it is now an antiques centre (with tea
rooms) and is only open at weekends.

Cross the road, with care, and follow Broomhill La to reach a road
junction. Bear right here to reach a road fork. Take the left-hand branch
(Irons La), but after just a few yards turn left to go up steps to reach a stile.
Go over and cross the field beyond to reach a stile down a flight of stone
steps onto a lane. Turn right and walk through a property (Broomhill
House) to reach a stile. Go over and follow the edge of the field beyond
to reach another stile. Now maintain direction across five further fields,
all linked by stiles. At a metal kissing gate go left at woodlands, following
a hedge to another kissing gate. Go through and bear left to reach a stile,
beyond which is a basic bridge crossing a stream. Follow the path beyond
the stream to reach a lane down to a road.

Walk forward along the road to reach, after about 150yds, a stile on
the right. Go over and cross a field to a stile beside an oak tree. Go over,
cross a field and another stile, then cut across a field to reach a stile (also
beside an oak tree) onto a road. Turn left and follow the road for about
400yds to where it bends sharp left.

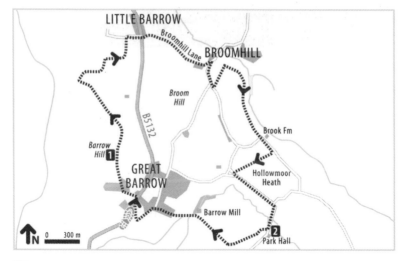

(2) Here, turn right down a lane towards the farm of Park Hall. Go into the field beyond the farm and cross it to a stile. Cross a field to a stile and go over into the field beyond. Maintain direction along this field until you can turn right over a basic bridge to reach a stile.

Go over and cross a field to a stile, crossing this and going down steps to a track. Turn left and follow the track, which becomes more substantial and acquires a name, Mill La, as Great Barrow is approached. Now bear left to return to the church.

Points of interest

Cheshire Plain: Geographically the largest part of the county is the Cheshire Plain, which stretches from Chester to Congleton. This superb agricultural area, occasionally drained as in the area north of Great Barrow, is one of Europe's most important dairy farming areas, the milk being used, in part, to make Cheshire cheese.

Stanlow: It is almost impossible now, when viewing the huge oil refinery at Stanlow, to imagine that in the twelfth and thirteenth centuries this was the site of an important Cistercian Abbey. The monastery was almost destroyed by storms and the monks moved to Whalley.

Ellesmere Port: This town, too, has changed radically, the Victorian seaside resort being replaced by an industrial complex and the opening of the Manchester Ship Canal.

Great Barrow: The village church, dedicated to St Bartholomew, has a superb red sandstone font, a fitting reminder of the area's geology.

Guilden Sutton & Christleton

START Guilden Sutton parish
car park, GR SJ449 683

DISTANCE 5 miles (8km)

MAPS OS Landranger 117
Chester & Wrexham; OS Explorer
266 Wirral & Chester

WHERE TO EAT AND DRINK
The Bird in the Hand, Guilden Sutton,
T01244 301753; The Ring O' Bells,
Christleton, T01244 335422

An easy walk through fields and across a golf course.

From the car park turn right, passing The Bird in the Hand. Just beyond
the pub turn right at the green marker post and go up some steps between
trees. At the top go through onto a metalled footpath at the rear of
some houses.

① Follow this path, keeping woodland on your left, to emerge between
houses into Belle Vue La on a sharp bend. Go ahead and after 400yds turn
onto a wide farm track on the left. Follow the track past a house and then
bear slightly right into a passageway hedged on one side by conifers. Cross
a stile at the end of this and a hedge. On the far side of the field, cross
another stile and turn right onto a lane. The lane reaches a metalled road.
Turn left along the road to its junction with the A51. Go straight across
towards the village of Littleton. After ½ mile turn right into Pearl La
towards Christleton and after 200yds take a footpath on your left through
a metal gate. Follow a well-defined footpath towards Christleton church,
crossing two fields. Continue along a passageway beside the church.

② Follow this to the main street of Christleton. Turn left along Pepper
St with its many attractive Georgian-style houses. At the village green
with its old pump and stone trough, turn left again and pass The Old Hall
on your right. Follow the road around to a large village pond, a beautiful
spot and a haven for all sorts of wildlife and birds. Just past the pond take
a footpath on the right. At the house bear right and go through a gap in
the hedge. Bear right here along a hedge and through two fields. Go past
a pond hidden by trees, then over a footbridge and through a gap in the
hedge. Keep straight ahead, then bear slightly left to cross another stile.
Bear slightly left again to reach a metalled road.

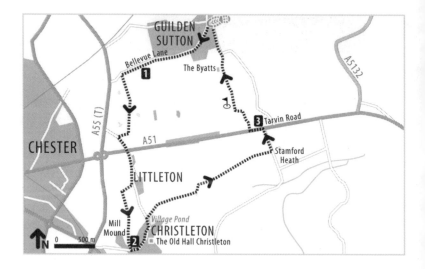

③ Turn left along this to its junction with the A51. Cross and turn left towards Chester. After about 100yds take a footpath on the right, going through a metal gate beside a golf clubhouse and, keeping that on your left, go around the back and follow the blue marker posts. Beyond a green, cross a fairway to the hedge opposite and a sign over a stile. Go over to a field and cross to another stile. Go through a small kitchen garden to a track beside a farmyard. Cross another stile to the lane ahead. At the next junction bear left into Guilden Sutton. At the junction in the centre of the village, where the road swings to the right, turn left to return to the car park.

Points of interest

Christleton: This large, sprawling village is full of interesting and impressive houses, dating from the mid-seventeenth century onwards. Christleton Hall has its own gazebo, an unusual summerhouse built into the garden wall, so that the ladies of the house could watch coaches going by.

The Old Hall, Christleton: This dates from about 1605 and is the oldest building in the village. During the siege of Chester in the Civil War, which lasted six months, this was probably the headquarters of the Parliamentarian forces. There is also a local tradition that the tunnel that encircles the whole building was at one time linked with Chester.

Knutsford & Tatton Park

START Car park in the centre
of Knutsford at the back of the
main street, GR SJ753 787

DISTANCE 5 miles (8km)
or 6 miles (9.5km)

MAPS OS Landranger 109
Manchester, Bolton & Warrington and
OS Landranger 118 Stoke-on-Trent
& Macclesfield; OS Explorer 268
Wilmslow, Macclesfield & Congleton

WHERE TO EAT AND DRINK
There are many cafés and pubs
throughout Knutsford and Tatton Park

Route 57 (5 miles/8km)
Some cobbled surfaces in Knutsford. Tatton Park is muddy in parts.

Leave via Malt St and turn right into King St, past the Heritage Centre
on the left. After 250yds take a path that bears right into Tatton Park, and
follow alongside the main drive for just over a mile.

① Pass by the cattle grid to the right and bear left along the drive to
Melchett Mere, ignoring the stile on the left. Go ahead a few yards past a
clump of trees and take a grassy path bearing to the left around the mere,
on the far side of the water. Continue on this path until you reach the gate
at the head of the mere. Take the grassy path to the right, to go diagonally
over parkland to join the drive again.

② Rejoin King St where you turned off for Tatton Park, and turn left
down Drury La past the Ruskin Rooms and a water tower further down
the hill. Follow the road around to the right along Moorside (noticing the
unusual buildings, the work of R. H. Watt), until it rejoins the far end of
King St near the railway bridge. Turn back right along King St where there
is a group of seventeenth-century cottages next to the church wall. Go left
up Church Hill and turn right into Princess St. Continue along Princess
St, passing the Methodist chapel, and turn left through Canute Pl and past
the White Bear Inn to Gaskell Ave on the other side of the roundabout.
Facing The Heath, where races took place for 200 years, is a row of town
houses, including Heathwaite House and Heath House. Return to Canute
Pl and go left along Tatton St in front of the Lord Eldon pub. Carry on
past some terraced houses and turn right along a short path opposite
Drury La. Walk right, along King St, keeping to the right-hand side, to the
Gaskell Memorial Tower. Return to the car park by the passage opposite.

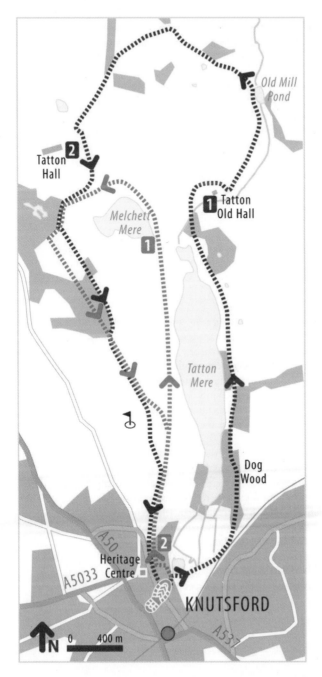

Old Mill
Pond

2 Tatton
Hall

Melchett
Mere

1

1 Tatton
Old Hall

Tatton
Mere

Dog
Wood

2

Heritage
Centre

A50

A5033

KNUTSFORD

A537

N   0   400 m

Route 58 (6 miles/9.5km)

An easy walk, fairly level through mature woodland and across open parkland. Some paths may be muddy after rain.

If you are a quick walker then the lay-by is free for 2 hours' parking, otherwise use the pay and display. Enter into the open park area (The Moor) by way of a gate in the railings, heading alongside a small pond on your left. Continue on the tarmac path, passing under the railway bridge, and continue to the park entrance. Enter Tatton Park by means of a tall gate and follow a footpath through the trees to the left; this will join the track you can see on the right a little further along. Emerge from the woods onto a track and follow this to the left, reaching another deer fence and gate. Bear right onto a gravelled track and follow this through the trees, passing a boat store yard on the right.

Follow the track or footpaths alongside the mere to walk into an area of car parking in some woods. Walk through to the far side of the car park woods and turn away from the lake towards some buildings in the trees (WC block).

[1] Bear right up to a metalled road, crossing Tatton Brook, and on your right is Tatton Old Hall. Follow the road around the Old Hall, and as it turns to the right bear left onto the site of an old medieval village with an information plaque. Follow the footpath across the fields as far as the old mill pond on the right, crossing a gravel drive and a small culvert, then bear left across rough ground towards a conifer plantation where the path is more distinct and runs parallel to a high deer fence. About ½ mile will bring you to the metalled road, the main way into Tatton Park.

[2] Turn left and walk alongside the road to a T–junction, where Tatton Hall and Gardens are on the right. Keep straight ahead with the metal fence on your right. Bearing right, you will pass the Temple at the end of the gardens; continue on a well-trodden grass path, passing Melchett Mere on your left, until Beech Ave is reached. The avenue is fenced off in places to prevent excess erosion by footfall, but the way ahead is clear, passing Knutsford Golf Club on the right, until you reach the metalled road near to the south entrance to the park. Leave through one of the side gates and after 50yds turn left along a short lane, which emerges onto King St in Knutsford. Walk along the main street until you reach the road leading down to the car park.

Points of interest

 Gaskell Memorial Tower: The walls are covered with quotations from well-known writers and there is a bust of Mrs Gaskell halfway up the tower.

Heath House: The home of Highwayman Higgins, who fraternized with the gentry and then robbed them. He was hanged in 1767.

Heathwaite House: Where Elizabeth Gaskell lived as a child with her Aunt Lumb.

Knutsford: See note to Walk 38.

Ruskin Rooms: Built by R. H. Watt around 1900 as recreation rooms for the laundry workers, whose cottages further down the hill he also built.

Tatton Hall: A grand mansion built in the neo-classical style for the wealthy Egerton family in 1813. Their extravagantly furnished and decorated rooms are well preserved, as are the servants' quarters, which give a fascinating insight into life behind the scenes.

Tatton Old Hall: This fifteenth-century building was the home of the lords of the manor, before the arrival of the Egerton family. The oldest part is the Great Hall with its high, carved, quatrefoil roof.

Tatton Park: A National Trust property owned by the Egerton family until the 1960s. The Park was landscaped by Humphry Repton in the late 1700s.

The Gardens: These were laid out in the 1850s and include exotic features such as a fernery, an orangery, a sunken rose garden and a Japanese garden complete with authentic Shinto Temple, shipped over from Japan.

The Heritage Centre: Built in the seventeenth century and now reconstructed.

The Lord Eldon: Home of Knutford's first May Queen, crowned in 1864. The landlord changed the name from the Duke of Wellington when the Duke supported the Catholic Emancipation Act.

Little Leigh & Barnton

START Little Leigh church,
GR SJ615 759

DISTANCE 5 miles (8km)

MAPS OS Landranger 118 Stoke-on-Trent & Macclesfield; OS Explorer 267 Northwich & Delamere Forest

WHERE TO EAT AND DRINK
The Beech Tree Inn, Barnton,
T07808 159375

A walk along the Trent and Mersey Canal near Northwich.

From the church walk westwards along the village street, heading towards Willow Green, but soon fork left off the road to follow a wide track. At the end of this maintain direction across a field, aiming for the left edge of a copse ahead. Follow a path along the wood edge to reach a road.

1   Turn left, soon going across a bridge over the Trent and Mersey Canal. On the far side of the bridge go down onto the canal towpath going left (south-east), following the canal past a bridge, then under power lines, then past Daleford House, to the right. Accompanying you along the path is the River Weaver, just a short distance to the right and running parallel to the canal.

2   Beyond Daleford House continue along the towpath to reach Saltersford Tunnel. Here, go up to reach the old horse path which goes along the top of the tunnel, going through another kissing gate and, further on, dropping down to reach the towpath again. Almost immediately, while on bridge 33, turn left onto a path and follow it to the A533 in Barnton.

Turn left, going past the Beech Tree Inn, and walk 300yds to reach Stone Heyes La on the right. Soon, the road turns sharply left; go with it, following it to reach Stone Heys Farm on the left. Just beyond the farm, go left over a stile and walk towards a powerline pylon. Go over a plank bridge and a stile and go along the edge of the field beyond to reach another stile. Go over and head towards Desley Heath Farm, going through the farmyard and continuing along the farm lane to a road. Turn left.

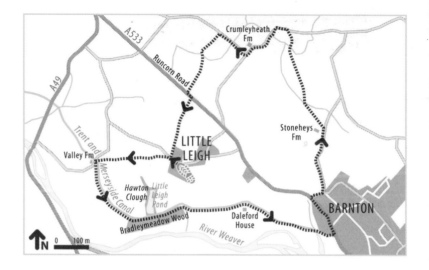

③ Ignore a turn to the right, going around a sharp left bend and continuing to reach Crumleigh Heath Farm on the right. Carry on past the farm and a chapel on the left for 400yds, past a row of houses, and at a footpath sign on the left, walk along a driveway and alongside the right of a house. Soon, go over a stile and cross the field beyond, keeping close to the hedge on the right. Go over a stile and cross a field to a stream. Cross, go through a gate and cross a field to a stile. Go over and follow a field edge to a stile onto the A533.

Cross, with great care, and follow the signed path opposite. Cross several fields linked by stiles, using the spire of Little Leigh church as a waymarker; your direction is to the right of this. When you reach a road, turn left along it to return to the church.

Points of interest

Trent and Mersey Canal: This canal formed part of the Cheshire Ring, joining the Bridgewater Canal inside the Preston Brook Tunnel. It links with the Shropshire Union Canal by way of the Middlewich Branch. In its commercial heyday, salt was one of the major items carried on the canal.

Saltersford Tunnel: Even though in the days of their construction horses pulled the canal barges – towpaths then really being used for towing – tunnels were not dug wide enough to accommodate the horses. The barges were then 'walked', the bargees lying on their backs with their feet on the tunnel roof. The horses had a short respite as they took the horse path over the tunnel.

Mottram & Broadbottom

START Mottram in Longdendale village green, by the Old Court House, M34 7NP, GR SJ993 955

DISTANCE 5 miles (8km)

MAPS OS Landranger 109 Manchester, Bolton & Warrington and OS Landranger 110 Sheffield & Huddersfield; OS Explorer 267 Northwich & Delamere Forest and OS Explorer 277 Manchester & Salford

WHERE TO EAT AND DRINK Various pubs and a small café in Mottram

Farmland, Pennine views, industrial archaeology and woodland. Muddy in places.

Cross the road and go through the car park to the right of the White Hart. Go over a stile and follow the track around to the corner of the cemetery. Go through a gate and walk along below the cemetery to reach a set of steps on the left. Descend, and cross directly to a double gate. Bear slightly left to another stile on the far side of the field. Cross the next field, following the right edge for about 100yds, dipping down on a muddy cow path to the stream. Cross here and up to the left is another stile. Over the stile follow the left side of the field down to the far corner, where there is another stile just before a house on the right. A narrow path runs alongside the garden fence, and out through a hedge onto a lane. Cross the lane and go over another stile into a field, bearing slightly right over a rise to a bridge. Look for the yellow footpath marker in the fence ahead, and turn right to a marker post.

[1] At the post turn right to follow the Etherow Goyt Valley Way. Follow the fence to the next field to a stile. Cross and keep to the hedge on the left until a farm track is crossed. Go over a stile, cross a field to another, then head uphill to a marker post. Take the right path uphill marked by a Tameside Trail sign, which leads past Pear Tree Farm and out onto Pingot La. Keep right along the lane, signposted to Broadbottom, with many cottages to walk past, and after passing under power lines you will reach a signpost to Hague La and a stile on the left. Go down the field, keeping to the left side, and reach a muddy path down to the lane.

[2] Turn right and follow it down to Broadbottom. Cross the road and go left under the railway arch, and immediately take the path to the right of the community centre. Go down steps to Mill Brow, and at the bottom turn right onto Well Row and walk down by the terraced houses to the end. There is a signpost to Hodgefold, up a rocky muddy path to the right.

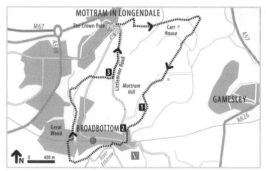

Stay along the route of this path which comes out onto Hodge La, passing cottages on your right. Follow the lane and you will arrive at the renovated Dye Vats on the left of the track. At the far end of the track at Hodge Fold Cottages and at the signpost for 'Hurst Clough via Great Wood', turn right. Follow a stream to steps leading up to the left. At the top, turn right, and go through a gate and follow a path through woods to a railway bridge. Go over and turn right to follow the railway until the path forks left to follow the brook far below to your left. This is Hurst Clough.

The path slowly descends the hillside to the brook, crosses it, and then re-crosses it. Take the second path on your right that leads uphill. This bends back to the left and leads, via a right fork, back to the brook again. Some distance later, cross the brook and take a right fork upwards, where steps will take you up out of the Clough. Once out of the woods follow the path gently upwards, keeping right up to Broadbottom Rd. Cross the road, and pass through a gate to the left of the building.

③ Follow the path, beneath the power cables, via three stiles onto Littlemoor Rd. Turn left and follow the road to the church on your right. Bear right to the church and before the gate, turn left down a cobbled path, then follow the church boundary wall to the right. After a grassy path and some more cobbles, a flight of steps leads back down Church Brow to the Crown Pole where you started out.

Points of interest

Summerbottom Cottages: Broadbottom was an industrial village, the River Etherow turning waterwheels. Summerbottom Cottages are handloom weavers' cottages, survivors of a period where entire families would work on the raw materials distributed to homes.

Mottram church: Stop and read the inscription on the tombstone of fifteen-year-old Lewis Brierley, buried in 1827: 'Though once beneath the ground his corpse was laid, for use of Surgeons it was thence conveyed...'

The Crown Pole: Erected in 1925 to replace an earlier wooden one.

Stretton Mill

START Stretton Mill (parking at the watermill only operates when the mill is open; there are spaces at a lay-by 100yds west of the mill), SY14 7JA, GR SJ454 430

DISTANCE 5 miles (8km)

MAPS OS Landranger 117 Chester & Wrexham; OS Explorer 257 Crewe & Nantwich

WHERE TO EAT AND DRINK The Cock O' Barton Inn, Barton, T01829 782277

A walk linking three pleasant villages and an old mill.

From Stretton Mill continue eastwards along the road, crossing the Carden Brook, which feeds the mill's pond, and continuing to the hamlet of Lower Carden. Here the road reaches a junction beside an imposing gatehouse. A few yards past this is a drive on the left that leads to Windmill House. Follow the track past a nice section of oak wood and carry on, passing the golf clubhouse on your right. Walk straight ahead on the track but bear right just before impressive sandstone outcrops. Keep to the track marked by the yellow waymarkers through the golf course.

[1] On leaving the course, the path continues downhill through a narrow woodland and then opens up leading to three houses, one being the 'Old Forge'. Go past this to reach the A534. Cross with care and walk down the road opposite. This is Clutton village. Just before a right-hand bend and just beyond the fine sixteenth-century black-and-white Charity Farm, turn left down a track. Go through a gate into a field and bear half-right to another gate, going through the next gate and then another field before a stile and small wooden bridge. Keep the hedge on the right and follow around to a track directing right towards the farm. Carry on to the lane and turn left towards Coddington.

[2] Cross over Coddington Brook, then just before reaching the village church, to the right, go left on a signed path. Cross a stile onto a lane and turn right along it. Opposite the pond is Whitegate Farm. On its left is a track; follow this past the farmyard, then go over a stile into a field. Go along the field's left edge and cross into another field and over another stile and another field. Now bear right; continue to reach a double stile in a hedge. Go over and cross the field beyond to reach a stile. Go over and cross the field beyond to reach a road.

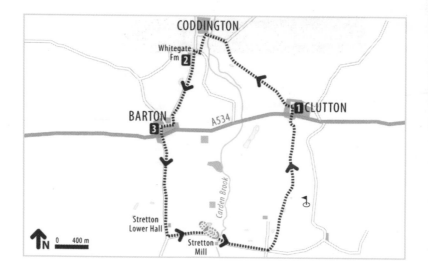

③ Turn right into Barton to reach a T-junction. Turn left and walk down to the main A534. Cross, again with care, and follow the road opposite, passing The Cock O' Barton Inn to the left. Follow the road past Stretton Lower Hall, to the left, then turn left on a road for Stretton Mill. Follow this road back to the start.

Points of interest

Stretton Mill: This is the oldest mill in Cheshire, dating from the sixteenth century.

Timbersbrook & The Cloud

START Car park at Timbersbrook picnic area, CW12 3PP, GR SJ895 629

DISTANCE 5 miles (8km)

MAPS OS Landranger 118 Stoke-on-Trent & Macclesfield; OS Explorer 268 Wilmslow, Macclesfield & Congleton

WHERE TO EAT AND DRINK Nowhere on the route, but The Coach and Horses, T01260 273019, is 1 mile south of Timbersbrook, going towards Congleton, and The Church House is at Buxton Rd, Buglawton, T01260 272466

An easy walk on good paths with some climbing and road walking.

Turn right out of the car park and after about 600yds go right again down Acorn La. At the end of the lane go straight over the crossroads and up Gosberryhole La and, as you pass a group of buildings on the right, the track narrows and bears to the left. Keep left when the path forks at a National Trust sign and continue climbing steadily upwards. At the brow of the hill there are good views to the left over the Cheshire Plain towards Jodrell Bank radio telescope and Alderley Edge. The path enters a wood at a low stone wall and at the junction of four paths.

1 Follow the path on the left marked for Cloud Summit, climbing, with the wood on your right for part of the way, to the top. From the trig point on The Cloud the views are magnificent. Leave the summit (you are now briefly in Staffordshire) and follow the main track in a south-east direction down some steps and to a farm track. Turn left and continue down the track to a road.

2 Turn right and walk along this pleasant minor road through the hamlet of Cloud Side for almost 1 mile, ignoring the road on the left signposted to Woodhouse Green. Shortly afterwards, where the road forks, keep right and continue round to a T–junction. Beware of fast cars as you turn right onto a main road for 250yds.

3 Turn right again at Bridestones Estate Farm and walk down the farm road to the burial chamber on the left.
    Retrace your steps to the main road and turn right, then right again after 100yds when you see the summit of The Cloud directly in front of you. The road bends sharp left at Springbank Farm.

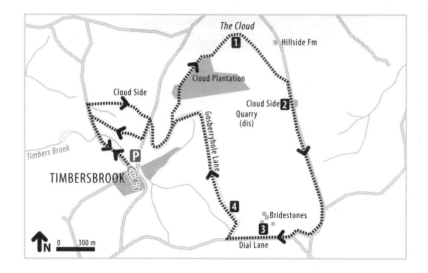

④   About 100yds later, it bends sharp left again along Gosberryhole La; follow this back to woodland, bearing left on entering the woods and following it around until reaching some steps that take you down to the road. Almost opposite is a track leading down to a farm. Walk through the farmyard onto a track that leads to the main road. Turn left and retrace your steps to the car.

Points of interest

The Cloud: To the north-north-west is Bosley Reservoir and, beyond it, Sutton Common radio mast. The cone-shaped hill to the right of the mast is Shutlingsloe. Rudyard Reservoir lies to the south-east and in a south-south-west direction beyond Congleton Edge are Mow Cop, Biddulph and the Potteries. On a clear day it is possible to see the Liver Building in Liverpool to the north-west.

Burial Chamber: A Neolithic site. The chamber is 18.5ft long and is divided into two sections. The semi-circular platform can still be seen. Two smaller chambers were removed in the eighteenth century.

63
64

Wincle & Sutton Common

START Wincle church, GR SJ959 661

DISTANCE 5 miles (8km)
or 10 miles (16km)

MAPS OS Landranger 118 Stoke-on-Trent & Macclesfield; OS Explorer 268 Wilmslow, Macclesfield & Congleton

WHERE TO EAT AND DRINK
The Ship Inn, Wincle, T01260 227217; The Ryles Arms, Hollin La, Higher Sutton, T01260 252244

Superb walking near the Staffordshire border.

From the parking spot down the quiet lane beside the church walk back up to the church and T–junction and turn left. Walk down the road to reach a turning on the right. The route continues along this road, going around a sharp right bend and then around a more gradual right bend. Just before reaching Wincle Grange Farm turn left through a gate and walk between farm buildings into a farmyard. Go through a gate and go downhill, eventually following a hedge on your right, to reach a stile. Now go through a gate on the right and turn left, continuing to descend.

1 When you reach a stream turn right and cross a bridge; follow the yellow waymarkers uphill to ruined farm buildings and carry on uphill to the top of Wincle Minn, turning right onto a lane. Follow this (the Gritstone Trail) all the way to the main A54 road.

The shorter route turns right, following the main road with care for about 600yds to rejoin the longer route, which reaches the A54 along the lane from Brooms Farm. (See final paragraph for the last part of the walk.)

The longer route turns left, also with care, then crosses the road to go over a waymarked stile on the right. Follow the hedge beyond to a stile.

2 Go over and follow the clear route towards the mast on Sutton Common, going over one more stile. Beyond the mast the Gritstone Trail continues along the ridge, bearing right after about 1½ miles to descend to a road.

3 Turn right, but after crossing a stream turn right along the drive to Kinderfields Farm. There is slight confusion now as the farm marked as Redwood on the OS maps is called Rossenclough locally. However, the track to it from Kinderfields is clear and obvious.

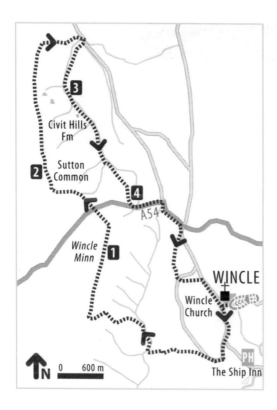

Continue onwards beyond Rossenclough, continuing to Civit Hills Farm. Go over a cattle grid and go to the left of the farm, going through a gate and following a stream to a gate past a pond on the left. Continue to follow the stream, going through another gate. Soon the path bears away from the stream, continuing uphill beside a hedge. Go over a stile and maintain direction to pass through Higher Pethills Farm.

4   Just before a cattle grid leading to a lane, at Pethills Farm, turn right through a metal gate and over a bridge to Brooms Farm. Bear right of this, joining its drive and following it to the A54 where the shorter route is rejoined. Turn left.

Both routes: continue along the A54 for about 400yds past the drive to Butterlands Farm, to the right. At the first turning on the right, turn for 100yds and take a stile on the right and follow the path over several fields to a lane. Cross and go straight over two fields towards another lane, turn right and walk downhill back to Wincle church.

65 Wybunbury & Hatherton

START Car park by the recreation ground in Wybunbury, GR SJ697 499

DISTANCE 5 miles (8km)

MAPS OS Landranger 118 Stoke-on-Trent & Macclesfield; OS Explorer 257 Crewe & Nantwich

WHERE TO EAT AND DRINK The Red Lion, T01270 841261, and The Swan Inn, T01270 841280, both in Wybunbury; Dagfields Antiques and Craft Centre, T01270 841336, and The Boars Head, T01270 841254, both in Walgherton

A pleasant walk in varied scenery.

1 Leaving the car park at its entrance, turn right and walk through the village towards the church. Just past the church turn left along Wrinehill Rd, passing Cobbs Moss on the left. Walk for about ¾ mile to Cobbs La and, directly opposite, turn right onto a bridlepath. Carry on along this for ¾ mile until you reach the A51. Turn left for 100yds then right, crossing with care. Follow a footpath sign along a lane, but before the next building take the stile on your right and head diagonally left across the narrow field to another stile. Go over, turn left, and through a gate to reach a footbridge. Bear right, walking uphill to the corner of a field, and then across two more fields to reach a lane.

2 Turn right and walk for ¼ mile to the B5071 and turn right again to Dagfields Crafts and Antiques Centre. Approximately 200yds past the antiques centre turn left up the track towards Oat Eddish Farm. Just before the farm turn right over a stile across to a small footbridge. Go across the field in the direction of Wybunbury Tower (see note to Walk 29). Go over this and cross the next field, leaving a dry pond on your left. Cross a fence and head towards farm buildings, crossing a tiny stream via a footbridge. Follow the left-hand field edge to the farm, then cross to a small gate onto the A51. Go right for 100yds (the Boars Head is 200yds straight on), then left by a black-and-white thatched house. Follow the field edge, always keeping to the left, and where the field dips down go through a gap and across a narrow strip to a stile. Go over this and diagonally right to a metalled lane. Go right to the B5071 and left over the bridge back to the start point, passing the Swan Inn.

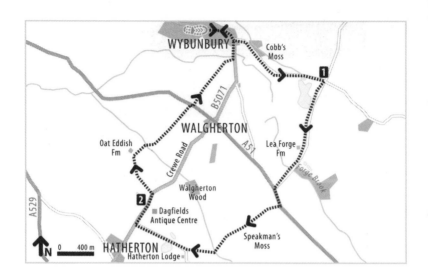

 Cobbs Moss: A protected area of reeds, bog, floating vegetation and trees – rich in plants and bird life.

Bunbury & Bunbury Locks

START Car park behind Trinity
Methodist church, Hurst Cl,
Bunbury, CW6 9QZ, GR SJ565 577

DISTANCE 5¼ miles (8.5km)

MAPS OS Landranger 117
Chester & Wrexham; OS Explorer
257 Crewe & Nantwich

WHERE TO EAT AND DRINK
Tilly's, T070 9330 2398; Dysart Arms,
T01829 260183 (both in Bunbury)

A lovely amble around a charming village and a length of the Shopshire
Union Canal.

From the large car park behind the Trinity Methodist church, walk back
down Hurst Cl to the junction with the main road and turn right. After
50yds a road sign directs you to the A49 and Tarporley; follow this road
but after 40yds turn right along a lane beside the Horse and Groom pub.
After 100yds turn left through a gate by a footpath sign and cross a field.
On the other side a gate takes you onto a path to a lane; turn left. Note
opposite is the Chantry House, a black and white timber-framed building
dated 1527.

1️⃣ Continue along the lane, bending towards the impressive church.
Opposite is the Dysart Arms Inn. Walk ahead and turn right but after
50yds turn left over a stile into the cemetery. (Please note a short detour
along this lane would take you to Bunbury water mill.) Walk ahead
through the cemetery to another stile, bearing left over a field to reach a
stile onto a lane. Turn left and follow, going straight ahead at a crossroads.

2️⃣ After ½ mile you cross a railway bridge and the lane bends sharply
left to the Shropshire Union Canal at bridge 106, Tilstone Lock. Turn
right onto the towpath and follow it past Bunbury Locks at bridge 105 and
continue towards the next bridge, 104.
    50yds before bridge 104 turn right through a metal kissing gate and
across to a small wooden bridge, through two more metal kissing gates
to a third one beside a telegraph pole. Bear right, heading towards the
church tower in the far distance. Go through a metal gate and across a
bridge, keeping the hedge on the left to another wooden bridge. Go over
and bear right to a stile between two metal gates. Go over and turn left,
walking for ¾ mile, ignoring three marked paths on the left and taking the

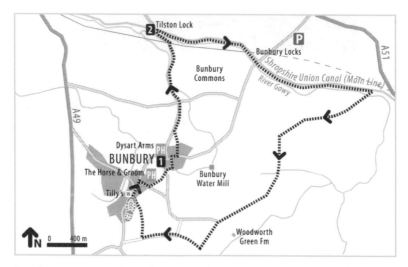

fourth opposite a sign for Birds La. Keep the hedge on your left and follow to a stile. Cross and walk straight ahead with the hedge on your right to a metal gate, going through and crossing two more fields and two more gates to a path between high hedges. After 50yds a gate entrances a field on the right; follow the path across four more fields back to the start.

START Acton car park, near the
Star Inn, CW5 8LD, GR SJ632 528

DISTANCE 5¼ miles (8.5km)

MAPS OS Explorer 257
Crewe & Nantwich

WHERE TO EAT AND DRINK
Waterside Café at the Nantwich
Marina, T01270 748283;
Nantwich offers a wide variety
of places to eat and drink

An easy walk comprising two canals and a little field walking.

On leaving the car park, turn right along the footpath for about 150yds,
then turn right into Wilbraham Rd. Where the road turns sharp right,
there is path between houses to the left. Pass a small bungalow, to the
left, which leads to a field. Cross the field and over the canal bridge (note
the panel that identifies this place as being part of the Battle of Nantwich
between the Royalists and Cromwell's army).

[1] There are steps to the left of the bridge down to the Shropshire Union
Canal. Turn right onto the towpath and proceed for about 1½ miles to the
junction with the Llangollen Canal.

[2] Cross the canal by the bridge to the left onto the Llangollen Canal
and proceed up the Four Lock ladder. On the right is the Hurleston
Reservoir, which is fed by the Llangollen Canal. The section of the walk
from here to Swanley is about 2¼ miles long. The route passes under
seven bridges and past five locks.

[3] Passing under the last bridge (at Swanley), climb away from the canal
onto the road and turn right. Pass the road junction ahead and look, on
the right, for a stile in the hedge at about 150yds. Go over the stile and
go diagonally across the field to another stile in the hedge. Cross over
the stile, then the drive and another stile into a field. Continue along
the path and through two fields then over a road and into a drive signed
'Madam's Farm'. Keep to the hedge on the left, ignoring the right turn of
the drive, and over a stile into fields. The path is clearly identifiable and in
about ½ mile over three fields turn left onto a track (the Star Inn is visible
ahead). Return to the car park after passing the inn to the left.

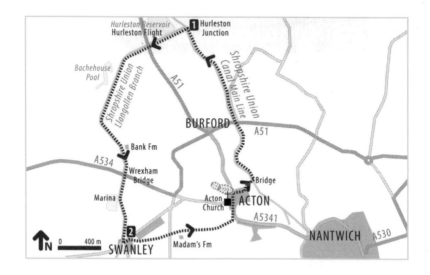

Points of interest

Bridge over Shropshire Union Canal: There is a sign showing an outline of the Battle of Nantwich.

Acton church: Recorded in the Domesday Book, this church has ancient origins. Its more recent claim to fame is that it was the Royalist headquarters during the Battle of Nantwich in 1644. (Nantwich Museum has a presentation of the battle.)

Aqueduct over the road by Malbank School: Made in cast iron, reflecting the impact of the Industrial Revolution.

Ackers Crossing & Mow Cop

START In the lane near Ackers Crossing, GR SJ850 589

DISTANCE 5½ miles (9km)

MAPS OS Landranger 118 Stoke-on-Trent & Macclesfield; OS Explorer 268 Wilmslow, Macclesfield & Congleton

WHERE TO EAT AND DRINK
The Rising Sun, Kent Green, Scholar Green, T01782 776235

A steady climb from the canal to Mow Cop.

Go over the crossing and turn right at the end of the lane to reach a canal bridge. Descend to the towpath by the steps at the far side.

① Turn right under the bridge and continue for about 1½ miles with extensive views of the Cheshire Plain on the right, then Ramsdell Hall on the far bank and Mow Cop in the distance on the left. At the road bridge, you can leave the towpath and turn right, walking along the pavement for 150yds to reach the Rising Sun pub, where refreshments can be sought.

Return to the bridge to continue the walk and continue along the towpath, leaving it at bridge 86, which you cross. Go under the railway and follow what looks like an old tram track running down to the canal. At the top of a rise you go into a wood and keep left through it. On leaving, cross two fields (walking close to the right-hand hedge because of boggy land) to reach a road. Turn left to the top of the hill and left again onto Chapel St. Beyond some houses and The Crown pub, the road dips and you will see the village hall on the right. About 300yds past this is The Brake, a narrow track leading uphill to a rough road. Continue on this, following the Gritstone Trail waymarker and footpath markers.

② Turn left along the road for 100yds to steps on the right leading up the side of the Memorial Methodist chapel to the village of Mow Cop. Facing the chapel is a short road leading to a T–junction, where you should turn left. Turn right immediately by the side of a three-storeyed building, which used to be a velvet mill. The path winds round the back of some houses, bears right, following the yellow marker post. The path curls around to Mow Cop Folly (see note to Walk 41), from where there are stunning views. Go alongside the right of it where a marker post directs you along the Gritstone Trail.

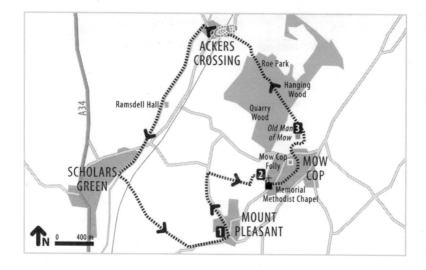

③ Following that, you eventually come to Wood La; cross and follow the signs for the Gritstone Trail opposite. Take this path, which leads to the west of the Old Man, and in a few yards a further sign points downhill to the left. It is worth stopping here to look at the unhindered view towards Congleton and the Peak District. Jodrell Bank radio telescope can also be seen on a clear day. Follow the downward path across a field and through woods to return to the lane from which you started.

Points of interest

Ramsdell Hall: A mid-eighteenth-century country house with unusual architectural features, including an octagonal dining room and a hexagonal hall. Privately owned.

Memorial Methodist chapel: Stands in Primitive St as a reminder of Mow Cop's part in the emergence of the Primitive Methodists as a separate sect. Camp meetings were held on the hilltop.

Aston Juxta Mondrum & Barbridge

START By the church in Aston
Juxta Mondrum, GR SJ652 568

DISTANCE 5½ miles (9km)

MAPS OS Landranger 118
Stoke-on-Trent & Macclesfield;
OS Explorer 257 Crewe & Nantwich

WHERE TO EAT AND DRINK
The Barbridge at Barbridge, To1270
528327 (popular canalside pub)

An easy, flat walk along part of the Shropshire Union Canal.

Facing the church go right (north-west) and take the metalled road on your left after a few hundred yards to a T–junction. Go over and take the gravelled lane to a stile. Go over this and cross over a railway bridge to reach a lane.

① Go along the lane and over several fields to reach the Middlewich Branch of the Shropshire Union Canal at Brickyard Bridge. Go over the bridge and left along the towpath for about 1 mile. The banks here are rich in wildflowers in the spring. Just before the Venetian Marina the towpath improves considerably.

② Pass the Marina on the left and continue for about 1½ miles to Barbridge Junction. Leave the Middlewich Branch of the canal at the junction and take the Wolverhampton Branch past the Barbridge pub to the bridge at Stoke Hall La. Access to the pub is over bridge 100.

③ Go left along the lane to reach Stoke Hall Farm at a left-hand bend. Follow a footpath sign to the right of the farm lane, going over a field and past the right side of a pond. Make for a stile straight ahead; go over it and head across to another stile, over a field to a small bridge and stile, then along a field keeping the hedge on your right. Go through a gate and immediately behind the gate over a stile through a small coppice and over another stile, crossing to another stile and a lane. Turn right for 150yds to a footpath sign and stile on the left opposite a farm. Go over across a field past a pond and towards large farm buildings, keeping to the right of the buildings to emerge onto a lane where you turn left past the farm to a fork in the road. Take the right fork to return to the start point.

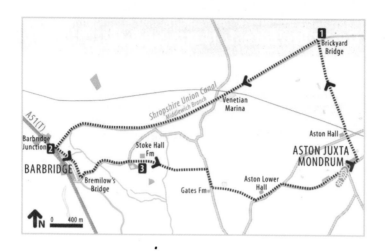

Points of interest

Venetian Marina: Here you will see an incredible array of watercraft, demonstrating the popularity of canal boating, if you needed convincing.

Barbridge Junction: Near the Marina there is a strange radio telescope apparently left over from World War II, when there was a tracking station and aerodrome at nearby Wardle, which played a part in the defence of Manchester.

Delamere Forest, Flaxmere & Hatchmere

START Barnes Bridge Gates
car park, GR SJ541 715

DISTANCE 5½ miles (9km)

MAPS OS Explorer 267
Northwich & Delamere Forest

WHERE TO EAT AND DRINK
Delamere Station Café T01606
889825; Delamere Café (in
the visitors' centre)

An easy walk that explores part of the forest and two of the local meres.

① Pick up the Sandstone Trail via a short path from the car park. Turn
left and follow this track for about 650yds. Just before a railway bridge
turn left onto another track. In about 500yds the track crosses a bridge
and in about 40yds turn left onto the Baker Way. This track leads to the
Forest Visitors' Centre (refreshments) in about 650yds. Continue past the
Centre eastwards and in about 150yds turn left over the railway bridge.
In about 50yds turn right into the woodland (note signs for Go Ape). The
path continues for about 450yds, where it joins the Delamere Way close by
Blakemere. Continue eastwards around the edge of the Mere for 250yds
and cross the B5152 into Whitefield car park.

② At the eastern end of the car park follow the Delamere Way for about
600yds (ignore tracks going off to the right) to the Forest edge and join an
old track. At its end turn left onto another track that leads to a path that
curves and rises to a gate. Keep to the path for about 150yds (through a
gate into a lane). Just before another gate, turn left through the hedge onto
a path.

③ Keep to the right and follow the path for about 450yds to a farmyard.
In about 50yds turn left over a stile onto a path. At its end turn left and
cross School La and into a lane opposite. In about 50yds turn right and
follow the track around Flaxmere for about 750yds. At this point the track
has now become a road and turns sharp right, leading to the B5152 and
opposite Hatch Mere.

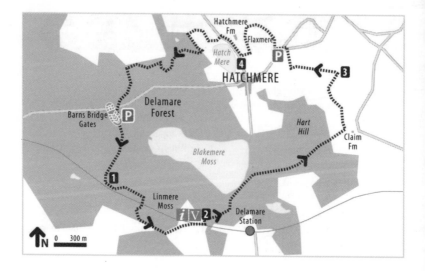

4 Cross the road and follow a narrow path parallel to the road. In about 250yds the path veers left and joins a footpath that follows round Hatch Mere. In about 600yds turn right over a footbridge, through a stile and up a steep bank onto a forest road. Turn right and follow the road for about 850yds to the edge of the forest, with a stile and footpath to the right. Keep on the track for about 500yds and arrive back at the car park.

Points of interest

Blakemere: Noted for its wildlife and birds.
Flaxmere: A Site of Special Scientific Interest (SSSI).
Hatch Mere: This is also a SSSI and is noted for its birdlife. It was created at the end of the last Ice Age by melting ice.

Grappenhall & the Lumb Brook Valley

START By the small church at
Appleton Thorn, GR SJ637 838

DISTANCE 5½ miles (9km)

MAPS OS Landranger
109 Manchester, Bolton &
Warrington; OS Explorer 276
Bolton, Wigan & Warrington

WHERE TO EAT AND DRINK
The Thorn Inn, Appleton, T01925
264362; The Rams Head Inn,
Grappenhall, T01925 213921; The Parr
Arms, Grappenhall, T01925 212120

A fairly level walk across fields, along a canal towpath and up a wooded valley.

From the church at Appleton Thorn, take Green La on the left and follow
it for about ½ mile. Beyond an old cottage, take the signposted footpath to
the right, going over a stile and following the hedge on your left to reach
a metalled road. Turn left along this, passing a junction and after 200yds
take a footpath on the right, following a hedge to a finger-post. Go over
the stile and bear left, following the field boundary around to the right
and to a marker post in the field. Turn left to the field edge and then right
at another marker along a footpath and over a small stream. Enter a large
field and head towards the woods straight ahead on the other side of the
field to the right-hand corner.

Turn left into the woods and walk through on a well-laid path to the exit,
where the path turns right passing a pond (old reservoir). Turn right
onto a track and follow this to a metalled road. Another right turn takes
you along the road for 400yds, where there is a footpath on the left into
Grappenhall Woods. Follow this path, bearing left to follow a line of
telegraph poles, with sign markers for the Mersey Valley Timber Trail.

1️⃣ As you approach the edge of the woods, the footpath narrows
between high hedges and fencing. At the end of this you will reach a
rough road beside the Bridgewater Canal. Turn left here and then again
onto a cobbled street through Grappenhall village. To your right are
ancient Grappenhall church and also a couple of pubs.

Follow the road to a junction and bear right to return to the canal.
Cross the bridge and turn left to find a gap in a hedge to drop down to
the towpath, turning right towards Stockton Heath. After about 1 mile

the canal crosses Lumb Brook Rd. Just before this, drop down right on a footpath with a metal handrail alongside and go left under the bridge. After about 100yds turn right and then immediately left to walk along the pavement. This is Dale La and the stream to your left is Lumb Brook. When the road begins to turn right away from the brook, carry on to the left along the pavement.

② You will come to a finger-post signed 'Dingle Lane', with the road sign showing the numbers 91–103. This is the start of the Lumb Brook Valley Park and the footpath winds through an attractive wooded valley following the stream. After about a mile you will reach a road that crosses the valley. Turn left, cross the bridge and continue upstream on the opposite bank. This next section is known as Fords Rough. After ½ mile you reach another metalled road. Turn right and immediately left onto a footpath, which is the end of Green La. Follow this back to Appleton Thorn and return to the start.

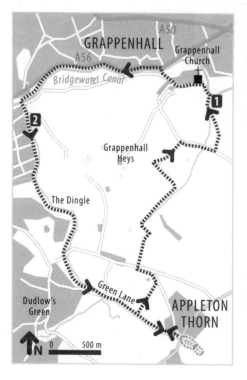

Points of interest

Appleton Thorn: A cutting from the Glastonbury Thorn, which is said to have sprung from Joseph of Arimathea's staff. On 29 June children dance around the thorn in a ceremony known as 'Barning the Thorn'. This has its origins in a pagan fertility rite.

Grappenhall church: A beautiful church dating mostly from the sixteenth century, notable for its ancient Saxon font and fourteenth-century stained-glass windows in the south wall. On the church tower is the figure of a cat with a grin, which may be the original Cheshire Cat.

Start Great Barrow
church, GR SJ469 684

Distance 5½ miles (9km)

Maps OS Landranger 117
Chester & Wrexham; OS Explorer
266 Wirral & Chester

Where to eat and drink
The Foxcote Inn, Little Barrow,
is now an Antiques Centre
and serves refreshments but
is only open at weekends

A gently undulating walk through farmland and along the course of a
Roman road.

From the car park, pass a telephone box and turn left into Ferma La. At a
junction keep straight ahead. Beyond Greysfield House the lane becomes
a rough track and bends right, gently descending with views left across the
Gowy Valley. After 400yds the footpath bears left, then right. At a junction
of footpaths with a metal gate, keep straight ahead going uphill. Where the
footpath bears right and left, go through a metal kissing gate on the right
and continue climbing beside a hedge.

[1] Follow the hedge around to the left and go down some stone steps in
the field corner to a farm road. Turn right along this to reach the B5132.
Opposite is the old Foxcote Inn, which is now an Antiques Centre and
serves refreshments (weekends only).

[2] Go left and then right into Broomhill La. Follow this to the hamlet
of Broomhill. Turn left at the next road junction. After 100yds take a
footpath on the right up a farm road. Go through the farmyard, turn right
beyond a gate and go through a metal gate. Keep ahead and go through
a series of metal gates marked with yellow arrows. After the fifth, veer
slightly left through a metal gate and footbridge, and reach a narrow entry,
which passes terraced cottages to emerge into Irons La. Turn left to a
junction with Barrow La.

[3] Turn right past The Old Farm and where the road veers sharply to
the right, take the farm road footpath on the left. Follow this towards Park
Hall, but just before reaching it, take a footpath on your right. (Do not
go through the farmyard, as shown on the map, as the footpath has been
diverted.)

Turn left along a hedge and at a gate, cross a stile and turn right along the other side of the hedge to reach a step stile. Cross this and go left. After 50yds turn left through a gate and then right along the opposite side of the hedge. After 400yds you reach another step stile, which crosses a ditch. Turn right to reach a stile in the corner of a field. You are now following the course of a Roman road.

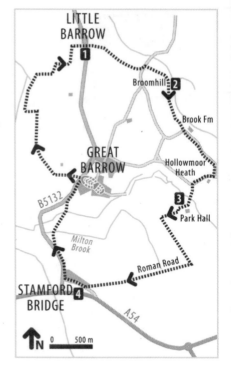

(4) Go over the stile and straight on beside the hedge, crossing two more stiles to reach a metal kissing gate out onto a road at the edge of Stamford Bridge. Go right to a T–junction in the centre of the village. Turn right along the B5132 and after the last house, take a footpath on the right through a kissing gate and bear slightly right along the hedge. Go past a cottage to a stile and footbridge. Cross these and head diagonally right across an open field in the direction of Great Barrow church perched on the hillside beyond. At the far side of the field a bridge leads over a brook to a stile. Beyond, a wide track climbs up to the B5132. Turn right along this into Great Barrow. Just short of the village, take a narrow lane right up to Great Barrow church. To return to the car park, follow the lane around to the left back to the B5132.

Points of interest

The Roman road: This was Watling Street North, which joined Chester to Manchester. Sections of the raised mound or agger on which the road was constructed can still be seen in the hedge.
Great Barrow church: This beautifully situated church is dedicated to St Bartholomew and dates from 1744. It has an interesting and unusual 'bull's eye' window and inside there is a register of rectors going back to 1313.

73 Harrow

START Lay-by on Tirley Lane
beside woodlands, GR SJ551 667

DISTANCE 5½ miles (9km)

MAPS OS Landranger 117 Chester
& Wrexham; OS Explorer 267
Northwich & Delamere Forest

WHERE TO EAT AND DRINK
Nowhere on the route, but outlets
in nearby Kelsall and Tarporley

A quiet walk, with lovely views, through forest and along a section of the
Sandstone Trail.

From the parking spot turn south (straight ahead) along Tirley La and
follow this road down to Quarrybank village. From the crossroads beside
the school turn right along the road to reach a T–junction.

1 Turn right through the last houses of Quarrybank and after about
250yds go left over a waymarked stile. Cross to woodland with ponds
and, keeping the hedge on your right, cross two fields before turning right
along a field edge (along this part of the route Beeston Castle is visible
to the south) to eventually reach a lane. Turn left onto the lane, passing
Rock Farm on the left, and soon after turn right on a track to follow the
Sandstone Trail northwards.

2 This is a delightful section of the Trail, going through a fine copse.
When a road is reached after ¾ mile, turn left along it, but after a few
yards go right on the signed Sandstone Trail. The Trail waymarkers now
guide you across fields into the most southerly section of the Delamere
Forest. As you enter the forest, turn right, then left to follow the electricity
poles to another stile.

3 Go over and bear right across the field beyond to reach the A54. Turn
right, with great care, along the road for 500yds, then go right on a signed
path that climbs up Harrow Hill to reach the edge of Delamere Forest
again. The path now continues close to the forest edge, descending at first,
then climbing again to reach the road, which is the start.

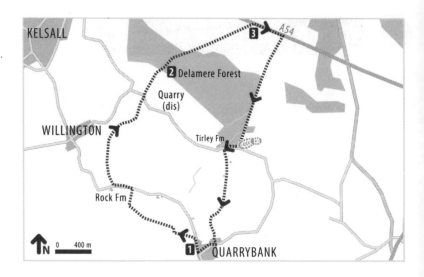

Points of interest

Beeston Castle: This fine old ruin dates from the mid-thirteenth century and was one of the main border strongholds during the Welsh rebellion. Later it was held by both sides during the Civil War. It is now in the hands of English Heritage.

Sandstone Trail: This 32-mile waymarked route links Beacon Hill, near Frodsham, to Grindley Brook near Whitchurch. It follows a high sandstone ridge, offering good walking and excellent views.

Delamere Forest: Today just 2,400 acres remain of a vast forest that once covered Cheshire from the Mersey to Nantwich. In Norman times Delamere was a Royal Forest, that is one in which only the king was allowed to hunt. The forest is now owned by the Forestry Commission, who have planted stands of pines among the ancient oaks.

Timbersbrook & Ravensclough

START Picnic area car park at
Timbersbrook, GR SJ896 627

DISTANCE 5½ miles (9km)

MAPS OS Landranger 118 Stoke-on-
Trent & Macclesfield; OS Explorer 268
Wilmslow, Macclesfield & Congleton

WHERE TO EAT AND DRINK
There are no pubs or cafés on the
route, although there are plenty in
Congleton; The Coach and Horses,
1 mile south of Timbersbrook
on the road to Congleton, has
stunning views over the Cheshire
Plain, T01260 273019

A strenuous walk with steep ascents over mixed terrain and splendid views.

Go through the picnic area, then up a flight of steps. Turn left on the road,
walk 250yds and turn into Gosberryhole La on the right. This leads to the
start of a steep hill called The Cloud (see notes to Walks 52 and 62).

① At the National Trust sign take the left-hand route, continuing
through woodlands and upwards to the summit of The Cloud. From the
trig point there are magnificent panoramic views over the Cheshire Plain
and Staffordshire Moorlands. Take the path that leads straight on and
continue past the National Trust marker down a flight of steps. At the
bottom, turn left and descend to a road. Turn left and after about 200yds
a small track leads off to the right to a stile with a small footpath sign.
Follow the stone wall over some board walks to a stile. Follow the marker
posts for the Staffordshire Way to a lane and turn right, following it to
Ravensclough Farm. At the farm go right along a marked footpath to the
right of the farm buildings. Follow the line of the telegraph wires to find a
stile leading into a wooded area with a steep ravine. This is Ravensclough.
The route through the clough is well defined. At the end of the path cross
a footbridge and go straight ahead with the river on your left. The river
soon forms a large loop.

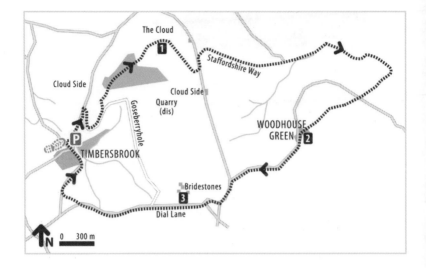

[2] At the end of the loop on a small ridge take an unmarked footpath to the right, keeping the hedge on your left, then climb the long grass slope to reach a road at the right of the farmhouse. Take the left-hand fork marked Woodhouse Green. At the end of the lane, by a telephone kiosk, turn left. At the next fork take the road to the left marked Biddulph. After passing a farm take a small road to the right, then go right again at a junction.

[3] Note the beautiful house and gardens here called The Bridestones. Follow the road to the county boundary, then take a footpath to the right. Do not enter the farmyard ahead, but go over a stile on the left into a field. Go straight ahead and follow the stone wall to a road. Turn right to return to Timbersbrook and the car.

Points of interest

Timbersbrook: A mill stood in the heart of the village and was used for silk production and dyeing from 1890 to 1976, when it was demolished. The mill pond is still there and can be seen when returning from the walk.

Start Walton Hall car park,
WA4 6SN, GR SJ600 852

Distance 5½ miles (9km)

Maps OS Landranger 108
Liverpool, Southport & Wigan and
OS Landranger 109 Manchester,
Bolton & Warrington; OS Explorer
276 Bolton, Wigan & Warrington

Where to eat and drink
The Hatton Pub and Grill, Hatton,
T01925 730314; The Walton
Arms, Walton, T01925 262659

An easy walk with one short climb.

Opposite the entrance to the car park is a bridge leading over the
Bridgewater Canal to Walton Hall. Beside the bridge, on the left, are some
steps; take these down to the canal towpath. Turn left and walk to the next
bridge. Leave the towpath at Houghs Bridge and cross the bridge onto
Houghs La. On the far side, take a footpath on the left, initially beside the
canal, but soon turning right away from it over a stile towards Hillfoot
Farm. Go through the gate, turn right through a cobbled yard, then left
at a finger-post, and turn left uphill beside a fence. At the top of the field
bear left to a kissing gate. Go through this and then another on the right
into a narrow, fenced pathway.

1   Continue past a cemetery to reach the top of Hill Cliffe. At the
crossroads ahead, turn right into Firs La and walk through a residential
area. After 400yds the road enters a deep rocky cut. About halfway along
this is the Wishing Well. Walk out of the cut and at a junction turn left
past Bellfield Farm ('Private Drive' sign applies to cars, not pedestrians).
The track veers around to the right, goes through a gate and past a large
house. Beyond the house, leave the track where it bears right. A finger-
post to Hatton points left; carry straight on along a grassy lane. Cross a
stream and climb out of the woodland to emerge into open fields; follow
a broad track with a hedge on your left. Go through a gap in the hedge to
where the footpath narrows and passes a wood with ponds in it.

2   From here a well-defined path crosses several fields to reach a gate,
which gives access to a rough road. Go straight on into the centre of
Hatton. A left turn at the junction with the B5356 leads to the Hatton Pub
and Grill, but the route goes right (towards Warrington). After ½ mile

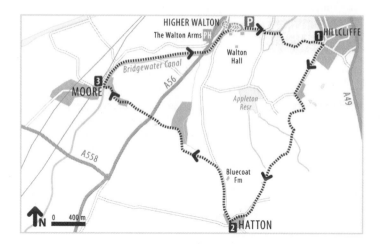

take the second path on the left, leaving the road over a stile to the left. A short distance in the field, turn right over another stile. Bear diagonally left across a field, go through a wide gap and then walk beside a ditch, to reach a stile into Rows Wood. Go over and through the wood, crossing a footbridge over a tiny stream. Climb the hillside opposite and turn right along the edge of the wood, which eventually bears left. Near a footbridge leave the wood and go ahead across a field, then bear left to a signpost on the edge of more woodland. Turn right here down to the A56.

③ Cross the road carefully into Hobb La and follow this into the village of Moore. Go over a canal bridge and then left onto the canal towpath. Turn left along the towpath to go back under the bridge and follow this for 1½ miles to return to the steps back up to the car park.

Points of interest

Walton Hall: The hall is an Elizabethan revival house, built in 1836. It was the former home of the Greenhall family, founders of the Greenhall Whitley Brewery in Warrington. The hall and gardens were given to the people of Warrington in 1941. The gardens are now a Country Park.

Hill Cliffe: A good viewpoint over Warrington and the surrounding area. To the west is the Runcorn–Widnes Bridge and Fiddlers Ferry Power Station. To the north, the slender spire of Warrington parish church can be seen with, in the background, Winter Hill and its transmitter.

The Wishing Well: An old horse trough, cut into the rock of a deep cutting, which was the old Chester Rd. It is fed by a natural spring and during the last century became known as a wishing well.

START Winterley Pool, CW1
5TR, GR SJ747 570

DISTANCE 5½ miles (9km)

MAPS OS Landranger 118
Stoke-on-Trent & Macclesfield;
OS Explorer 257 Crewe & Nantwich

WHERE TO EAT AND DRINK
There are no pubs or cafés on the
route but the following are nearby:
The Hawk Inn, Crewe Rd, Haslington,
T01270 582181; The Fox, Crewe
Rd, Haslington, T01270 584934

A very peaceful, easy-to-follow walk.

Walk to the Crewe side of Winterley Pool and into the lane on the left. At
the start of the lane go into a field at a footpath sign on the right. Continue
through several fields and over stiles until two farms come into view; bear
left towards the farm on the left and go over the stile, crossing over a lane.

1 Take the footpath over a stile straight ahead. Note the beautiful half-
timbered Haslington Hall amongst the trees to your left. Cross the farm
drive and take the track, which is signposted straight ahead. The track
ends in a field where there are two footpath signs. Take the path straight
ahead, following a farm track for 200yds before reaching a field. Go
straight ahead beside a gate then through four more gates, emerging onto
a lane opposite house No. 85.

2 Turn left to reach Crewe Golf Club. On passing the entrance, carry
straight on at the footpath sign, following a good track to a footpath
marker post. Take the path straight on past a maintenance building and
to the left of a pond, and cross a path to enter a field through a gate in the
facing hedge. Go straight on to emerge onto a track, which leads to a stile
at the side of an iron gate on your left. Go over, turn right in the field and
go round to the right of the farm buildings. Go over a stile onto a concrete
track and turn right through the farmyard, avoiding the path to the
farmhouse, and leave by the driveway. Turn right on to Holmshaw La and
follow to a fork. Go left, and turn right at a house called Woodland View.

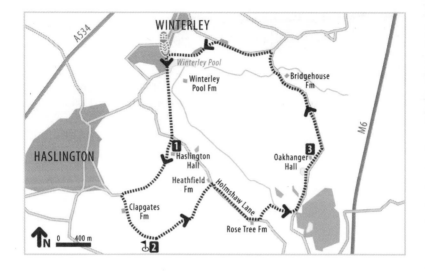

③ Turn left at a T–junction and enter the driveway of Oakhanger Hall. On reaching a pond, turn right across a stile and around the buildings to a stile over a track and over another stile opposite, crossing a field to the right-hand corner to a further stile. Go over, continuing straight ahead to a collection of stiles. Go straight on along a green lane to Bridgehouse Farm. Go straight through the farm and leave by the drive. Turn left onto the road and at the crossroads turn left again to return to Winterley, then left again back to Winterley Pool.

Points of interest

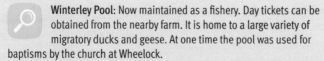

Winterley Pool: Now maintained as a fishery. Day tickets can be obtained from the nearby farm. It is home to a large variety of migratory ducks and geese. At one time the pool was used for baptisms by the church at Wheelock.

Haslington Hall: A well-preserved, half-timbered house built in 1585. It is a private dwelling and only open to the public for special events like weddings.

Circuit of Shutlingsloe

START By the bridge in
Wildboarclough, GR SJ982 687

DISTANCE 6 miles (9.5km)
or 12 miles (19km)

MAPS OS Landranger 118
Stoke-on-Trent & Macclesfield;
OS OL24 The Peak District

WHERE TO EAT AND DRINK
The Crag Inn, Wildboarclough, To1260
227239; The Hanging Gate Inn,
Haddon, Sutton, To1260 400756

A stunning walk around and over Shutlingsloe Moor.

Walk away from Wildboarclough south to the Crag Inn. At a footpath sign go through a gate and contour the hillside over stiles, with Shutlingsloe on your right and fine views across the Cloughbrook valley to your left. At a sign for path 379 turn up onto a lane leading from Higher Nabbs Farm. Follow this left to the road. Go down 150yds to the stream bridge and follow a track and stream right to a stone footbridge.

For the shorter version of this walk, turn right here and follow the course of High Moor brook. Eventually the path will bear left away from the brook. Follow the path and it will lead you to the slope of Nessit Hill, where you will rejoin the longer route, just after ②.

① Go over this and left up Oakenclough valley, passing the lovely farm buildings on your left. Go left up the hill, through several gates and stiles following the marker posts to exit at the Hanging Gate Inn. Go through the pub yard and down the footpath to a road. Go left for 100yds, then right onto the Gritstone Trail. Follow the Trail through several gates and fields for ¾ mile to Throstles Nest Farm.

② Walk left of the farm and, directly behind, take a path to the right into Macclesfield Forest, walking over a footbridge and up some steps to a finger-post just before the reservoir. Take the trail for No. 3 footpath along well-marked tracks, and after about 1 mile go over a stile onto open moorland. Follow the waymarked track to Shutlingsloe summit.

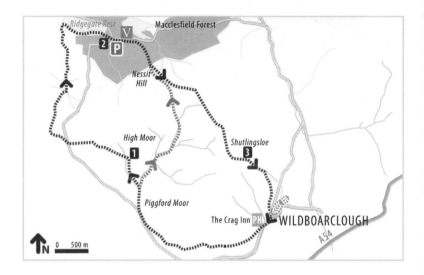

③ Descend the east side to Shutlingsloe Farm and a lane. Take the lane down right until you meet a road. Turn left to the start point.

Macclesfield Forest: This working woodland is a scenic blend of forest, lakes and moorland with plenty of wildlife. It was once a Royal Forest created by the Norman conquerors.

Darnhall & Wettenhall

START Darnhall village hall,
CW7 4DG, GR SJ634 632

DISTANCE 6 miles (9.5km)

MAPS OS Landranger 118 Stoke-on-Trent & Macclesfield; OS Explorer
267 Northwich & Delamere Forest

WHERE TO EAT AND DRINK
The Boot and Slipper,
Wettenhall, T07970 221112

A long walk along pleasant footpaths and quiet roads.

From the hall take the footpath opposite, along Smithy Bank Rd. Continue on along a driveway and bear left through a wooded area, following the track uphill out of the wood.

① Take the path to the left, which leads to the base of a radio telescope. A short distance before a gate, cross the field to your right to reach a stile. Go over and turn left to another stile. Go over and turn right, following the hedgerow on your right, through several fields until you reach a metal kissing gate on the right. Go through and carry on across several fields to a track by Woodside Farm. Cross over and turn left down the lane for ½ mile to a lane at Wettenhall Green.

② Turn right and walk ½ mile to the Boot and Slipper Inn. Continue along the same road to a left-hand bend with chevron marker and enter the field ahead of you. Cross to a ditch, going over where there is access, and up the field to a stile. Cross over to another stile right of the house ahead, being Wettenhall Farm. Cross over, going straight ahead and passing over a concrete path, then continuing straight ahead to another stile with the hedge on your left. Go over and bear left to a stile and carry on for several fields to a lane. Turn right back to the village hall and the start.

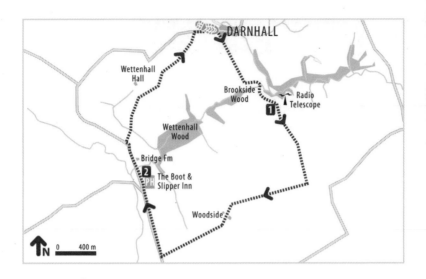

Points of interest

Radio telescope: One of a number belonging to the University of Manchester and controlled from Jodrell Bank. It is used to gauge the distances of astronomical radio sources on a triangulation basis in conjunction with others in Sweden and America.

Foxwist Green & Petty Pool

START Car park on the Whitegate
Way at Whitegate station,
CW7 2QE, GR SJ615 679

DISTANCE 6 miles (9.5km)

MAPS OS Landranger 118 Stoke-on-
Trent & Macclesfield; OS Explorer
267 Northwich & Delamere Forest

WHERE TO EAT AND DRINK
The Plough Inn, Foxwist
Green, T01606 889455

A walk that includes part of the Whitegate Way.

From the car park walk south-east along the Whitegate Way and follow
it for ½ mile until a sign directs you to the right gradually downhill to a
road. Cross over and take the footpath opposite, going over a stile and
ascending a short hill. At a farm, go right of the house to cross a stile onto
the farm drive. Turn right along the lane to reach a crossing lane. Turn
left. The Plough Inn is ahead, but the route goes right up a track to a stile.
Go over and go along the left edge of a field to reach another. Go over
and cross a field to a stile. Go over and descend to a footbridge. Cross,
go up the field ahead and turn right over a stile. Walk across to a gate, go
through and follow a holly hedge to a road.

Turn right to reach Swallow's Nest, turning left beside the drive. Go past
the house and through a gate. Cross a field to a stile. Go over and follow
the field edge to reach a gap at the bottom, on the right. Follow the right-
hand hedge, go over a stile and bear right to a stream.

①   Now ascend to reach Grange La and turn left into Whitegate,
following the lane to the church. Walking past the church, continue
along the road. After a few yards turn left into a car park and follow the
fishermen's path to New Pool. When the pool is reached, bear left to follow
its edge, with the water on your right. Go over a footbridge and bear left
into a wood. Walk along the wood edge and follow a length of boardwalk.
At the end of this is a gate into a field beside a thatched cottage. Go
through, bearing right to a track up to the cottage.

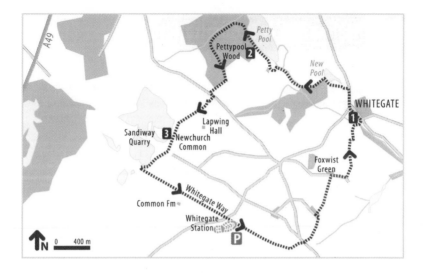

2 Just beyond this is a path on the right. This permissive path soon reaches Petty Pool. Bear left to follow the Pool, with the water on your right. Follow the water edge path into Pettypool Wood. As the path nears the outflow stream it bears away left, soon becoming a substantial forest track heading south-westwards. Ignore all side turnings from the track, following it to a road (Dalefords La). Turn left, then almost immediately right down a lane to Lapwing Hall Farm. Soon, go right on a signed path beside a holly hedge. Go over a stile and cross a field. On the far side turn left to reach a track. Cross the track to a stile and go over into a pine copse.

3 Walk through the copse to a rough lane, cross over and go straight ahead through trees beside the water-filled Sandiway Quarry, bearing right and onto the Whitegate Way. Turn left and follow the way under a road to reach the start.

Points of interest

Sandiway Quarry: The extraction of sand has created water-filled pits that are a haven for birdlife.

Whitegate Way: This short, 6-mile trail follows the track bed of the old mineral railway from Cuddington to Winsford.

Whitegate: St Mary's church was once a chapel of Vale Royal Abbey. Today it is the centrepiece of a picturesque village, with some thatched cottages adding to the general charm.

Hankelow & Broomhall

START Free car park in
Audlem, GR SJ659 437

DISTANCE 6 miles (9.5km)

MAPS OS Landranger 118
Stoke-on-Trent & Macclesfield;
OS Explorer 257 Crewe & Nantwich

WHERE TO EAT AND DRINK
The White Lion, Hankelow,
T01270 812462

A very pleasant walk along the canal, with fine views.

Leaving the car park in Audlem, turn left and after 50yds left again, just past the cemetery, walking along a lane called Moss Hall.

1 After 100yds go through a metal kissing gate on the left and walk across two fields, going through two more metal kissing gates to the Shropshire Union Canal and turning right onto the towpath, walking north past bridge 79 to bridge 82 at Austin's Bridge.

2 Turn right away from the canal and down to Coole La. Turn left and walk 200yds to a stile on the right. Follow the signs across three fields. Go through a gate and turn right down to another gate. Go diagonally right to a stile in the corner of the field. Go over and keep the boundary on your right to go over two stiles and then a cart bridge over the River Weaver. Follow a concrete slab track beyond the bridge until it reaches a stile after 200yds. Go over, with the boundary on your left, then go over another stile and follow the boundary on your right to a lane and turn right.

3 Walk down the lane and where it turns sharply at Ball Farm, turn with it and walk up the lane into the village of Hankelow. Bear right at the large village green to the A529. Turn right onto this and walk along the pavement for ¼ mile to a metal kissing gate on the left. Keep the boundary on the right and go along and through four kissing gates onto a driveway. Follow to a lane and turn left for 200yds, turning into a bridleway on the right, just after Mill House. Follow the track until it reaches another track, and carry straight on to reach Heathfield Rd. Go straight on but after 50yds turn right onto the A525 and follow it, walking around the church back into Audlem and the start point.

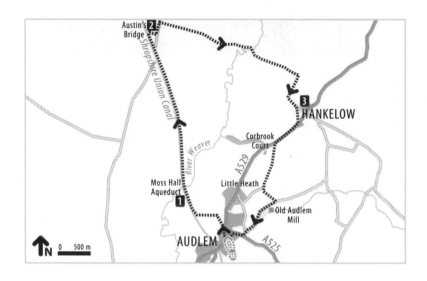

Points of interest

Audlem: A charming village with a fine church and several good pubs and hotels. It's also a canal holiday centre with a succession of locks.

Wildboarclough to Three Shires Head

START Peak National Park
car park at Clough House,
SK11 0BD, GR SJ987 699

DISTANCE 6 miles (9.5km)

MAPS OS Landranger 118
Stoke-on-Trent & Macclesfield;
OS OL24 The Peak District

WHERE TO EAT AND DRINK The Crag
Inn, Wildboarclough, T01260 227239

A gritstone walk near to the source of the River Dane, with some delightful picnic
spots and swimming holes.

Follow a broad track by Clough House signposted to the Cat and Fiddle
Inn up Cumberland Brook. Keep the woodland on your right and 150yds
past the end of the woodland go right on another track; this is footpath
No. 103 of the Peak Footpath Preservation Society. Follow this for ½ mile
until you meet the main Buxton Rd. Go directly across the road and down
some metal steps, across the field ahead and over a dry stone wall. Keep
the wall on your left and walk to a metal gate and turn right onto a track
leading downhill to another gate. Go through and turn immediately left,
following the yellow marker posts to the River Dane.

①   Follow the true right bank (Cheshire) of the river to the Pack Horse
Bridge and Panniers Pool at Three Shires Head. This is where Derbyshire,
Staffordshire and Cheshire meet. Follow the sandy track up right and away
from the river for ¼ mile until it is possible to cut down left across fields
to reach Knar Farm.

②   Follow the gated metalled road for 1 mile to a junction with a road.
Go right here past Midgleygate Farm and Burnt Cliff Top to the top of the
hill and a path on the right.

③   Follow the path across open country for about 1 mile until you reach
the main Buxton Rd. As the track sharply bends just before the main road,
drop down on the right to a stile and cross over the road, going over a stile
directly opposite. Head diagonally towards a lone barn. Turn left at the
barn to the top right of a wood, then cross over a stile and into a disused
lane at the left side of the next wood. Go down this lane and diagonally
left to another short lane. Turn left here for 100yds, then cross over a stile

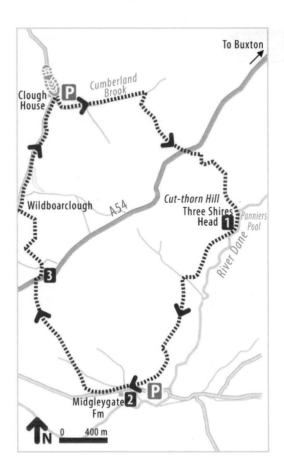

into a wood. Carry on down through the woods to cross a footbridge over Clough Brook just by the Crag Inn. Turn right here and walk along the road for 1 mile to regain the start point at Clough House.

Points of interest

Three Shires Head: This is the point where Cheshire, Derbyshire and Staffordshire meet. The River Dane is crossed here by a Grade II-listed packhorse bridge, which was part of an important trading route.

Dunham Park

START St Mark's church, Dunham Town, GR SJ740 879

DISTANCE 6 miles (9.5km)

MAPS OS Landranger 109 Manchester, Bolton & Warrington; OS Explorer 276 Bolton, Wigan & Warrington

WHERE TO EAT AND DRINK
Ye Olde No. 3 Inn, T01925 757222, on the route; The Swan with Two Nicks, Little Bollington, T0161 928 2914; The Axe and Cleaver, Dunham Town, T0161 928 3391; refreshments are also available at Dunham Massey Hall when open

From the church, which lies at the intersection of two roads, go north on the road for about 250yds, taking care over the narrow road bridge over the Bridgewater Canal. Cross the bridge and turn left down a path to the canal towpath. Walk along the canal path for the next 2 miles, and expect to pass many canal barges moored up along the way. Pass over an aqueduct on the B5160 and then another over the River Bollin. There are occasional views over to Dunham Massey to the left, and further afield to the Pennines in the distance.

1 Beyond the River Bollin go under three sets of power lines to reach Agden Bridge. Go under the bridge and turn right on the path up onto the bridge. Walking over the bridge turn left at the road junction, and continue on the 'No through road' to reach the A56. Take care crossing over the road here as it is busy.

2 Turning left, walk along the pavement until you reach a track opposite Ye Olde No. 3 Inn. Opposite the inn is a path through a kissing gate; walk along the field edge and you will reach a stile by a gate on the left. Go over the stile, and maintain the direction to reach another stile, which you can see across the field. Over the stile a grass track is reached. Turn left towards Arthill Farm, where the path passes through a jumble of buildings. When you reach the greenhouses, go to the right and follow the field edge to a stile in the field corner.

Cross the road and take the path beside Reddy Lane Cottage. Go over a stile and follow the field edge towards the wood ahead. Aim for the left corner and you will find a stile in the corner of the field, although you may have to go over a low fence on your left just before the stile. Go along the northern edge of the woods, keeping the trees on your right. When you reach a corner, turn left 90 degrees and follow the field down to a stile in

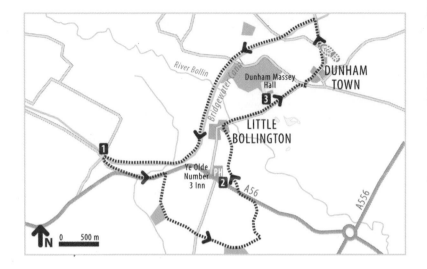

the hedgerow by a gate. Ahead is a white house; follow the field down to the house and the stile is on the right. Immediately over the stile turn left down a short grass lane to a stile and come out onto a lane. Turn left and follow the road to its junction with the A56. Turn left along the pavement to reach a group of cottages on the right at New Farm. Cross with care and there is a stile just at the back of the cottages, which may be overgrown. Go over the stile to follow the field edge to reach another stile onto a muddy track. Immediately across the track go over another stile into another field along the right edge and walk to the next stile. Over the stile and a path leads up to the Swan with Two Nicks Inn, Little Bollington.

Turn right along the lane to cross the River Bollin on a narrow footbridge with a weir on the right side and after the bridge the old millhouse on the left. Ignore the permissive path to the right and the lane to the left; carry on forward along a tree-lined track towards Dunham Park.

3 Enter the park over a wooden, stepped stile and pass Dunham Massey Hall on the left (ice cream available here). After the hall take the left fork of the path down a new lime tree avenue to reach another ladder stile out of the park, turning right. Cross the road carefully and turn left along the road to Dunham Town. Ignore the turn on the right and return along the pavement to reach the church at the start.

Points of interest

Ye Olde No. 3 Inn: Opinions may vary as to why the name of this Inn – once the Red Lion – was changed. Some say it was merely the third of Little Bollington's inns, which seems highly unlikely; others say it refers to its being haunted by three ghosts, which seems even more improbable. Yet others say it refers to the inn's coaching past, when it was the third stop on the Chester to Manchester run. That seems the most likely, but is rather mundane.

The Swan with Two Nicks Inn: No, this is not a misprint: it is 'nicks' not 'necks', the nicks in question being those made on the swans' beaks during the local 'swan-upping'. The inn was reputably one of Dick Turpin's favourite hideouts.

Dunham Park: A magnificent 250-acre deer park, in which fallow deer can frequently be seen, surrounds the eighteenth-century Dunham Massey Hall, once home to the Earls of Stamford but now in the hands of the National Trust. The Hall is open to the public and houses superb collections of furniture, paintings and silver. The mill, passed on the walk, is sixteenth century and is now private housing.

Adlington

START Lay-by on the A523 just north of The Legh Arms, Adlington, SK10 4NA, GR SJ912 806

DISTANCE 6½ miles (10km) or 7½ miles (12km)

MAPS OS Landranger 109 Manchester, Bolton & Warrington and OS Landranger 118 Stoke-on-Trent & Macclesfield; OS Explorer 268 Wilmslow, Macclesfield & Congleton

WHERE TO EAT AND DRINK The Legh Arms, Adlington, T01625 829211; Adlington Hall (serves teas when the hall is open); The Coffee Tavern, Shrigley Rd, Pott Shrigley, T01625 576370

An easy walk through fields, woods and along the canal towpath.

Leave the car park in the direction of The Legh Arms, turn left into Brookledge La at the crossroads and continue for 350yds to turn right into Wych La. Where the lane turns sharply right go down a track straight ahead. Where the track bends right go over a stile, cross a field to Harrop Green Farm and walk through the farmyard. 50yds beyond, cross over a stile on your right, keeping the hedge on your right until you reach a marker post that directs you to the left towards a stile by an oak. Go over and gradually bear left, uphill, to the left-hand corner of the field, going over a stile onto the Middlewood Way.

1. Cross directly over, over a stile into a field, following the path to reach the Macclesfield Canal at bridge 22. Take the steps on the left down to the towpath. Go left under bridge 21 some 100yds beyond, crossing the waymarked stile on the left. Bear right, over a field towards a stile in the trees. Go over and right to a second stile by a gate and over onto a road. Almost opposite is a marked footpath, which points along a track signed 'Springbank Farm'. Follow the track down towards a house. Go right, following a yellow marker, and skirt the house to a stile. Bear left, curling around to eventually traverse a wooden bridge over a stream, going over a stile and uphill to another, left of Jepsonclough Farm. Go over onto a tarmac drive. Turn left and continue to a quiet lane beside a gate marked Jepsonclough Farm and turn right, following the track to the canal and

going over the canal bridge. Pass through a caravan site to Woodend Farm, where a gate bars the way.

For the shorter route, when you reach Springbank Farm, turn right along Springbank La. Follow the lane, which will take you across the canal and through some woodland. As you leave the woods, turn left into Brookledge La, which will take you a T-junction with Norman's Hall Farm on your left. Turn right into Shrigley Road, which is where the shorter route rejoins the main route.

2   Take a path on the left and go over a series of stiles with the canal on your left to reach Adlington Basin. Go right past a few caravans and along a good track for 500yds to a property, keeping to the left of it and going over a stile, then another, before turning right. Go over a stile and bear left across a field towards the far hedgerow, eventually reaching a gate and coming out onto a lane. Go right for nearly ¾ mile, then bear left and at a junction bear left towards Bollington.

3   At the public footpath sign 200yds further on, turn right over a stile and then head left and downhill towards Styperson Pool. Cross a stile to enter woodlands, following a path left of a pool to join a drive and then a road. Go left for 225yds and then follow a public footpath sign on the right just before Winterfold Farm.

4   Cross the canal bridge, following the path down to cross one field and over a stile onto the Middlewood Way beside Higher Doles Farm. Turn left onto this and after 150 yards turn right through a metal kissing gate onto a track and turn left; where the track forks turn right at Whitely Croft. Go over several cattle grids and through gates until, just before a house, you turn left off the track. With a hedge on your right, reach and go over a stile next to a hedge gap and then under power cables. Turn right and keep to the left of a hedge to cross a stile. Turn left and cross a footbridge and stile ahead. Go right and, keeping to the edge of the field, cross a stile. Bear left and follow a path to a stile onto a farm track. Turn right to Wych La and the route back to the start.

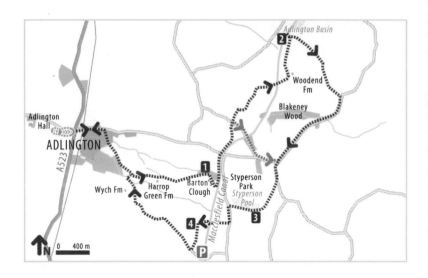

Points of interest

The Macclesfield Canal: Opened in 1831, the canal is 26½ miles long and was designed by Thomas Telford. It connects the Peak Forest and Trent and Mersey Canals.

START Wrenbury Bridge, GR SJ590 481

DISTANCE 6½ miles (10km)

MAPS OS Landranger 117 Chester & Wrexham; OS Explorer 257 Crewe & Nantwich

WHERE TO EAT AND DRINK
The Cotton Arms, T01270 780377, and The Dusty Miller, T01270 780537, both in Wrenbury

A delightful and rewarding walk, which at the right times can be rich in wildlife and wildflowers.

Follow the Llangollen Canal, a branch of the Shropshire Union Canal, westwards from the Dusty Miller for 1½ miles, with Marbury Brook on your left.

1 The obelisk on the left horizon is a monument in Combermere Park. At the first road bridge (No. 23), Church Bridge, leave the canal and go right for Norbury.

2 Go through the hamlet, bearing left and passing a converted chapel on the right. After 250yds on a road bend and just before a track is a footpath marker post pointing to the right. Follow this across three fields and three stiles, the last stile coming out onto a track next to a house. Bear left onto a lane.

At Moss La follow the lane all the way to a T–junction and turn right onto Common La. After 150yds go through a gate by a marker post. Follow the path to the right edge of a wood. Go through a gate and turn immediately right and follow the field boundary on its left. After a slight bend go through a gate and diagonally right past some oaks to a double gate. Go straight ahead, aiming for a point about 100yds left of the farm buildings ahead. At a minor road go left. Beyond the next farm on the right is a footpath marker post. Go over a stile and go straight across the field to a corner and follow the hedge round towards a corrugated red barn. Just before the barn go through a hedge and make for a gateway in front of a red house. Go right here on a minor road for 100yds to a footpath sign on the left. Go over a stile and make for a redbrick farm.

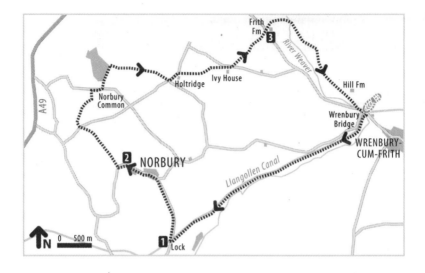

3　At Frith Farm go through the farmyard to exit at the rear of the buildings. Go right to a hedgerow and follow this down to the River Weaver. Cross the river by a cart bridge and go up the opposite bank to a hedgerow. Follow the hedge rightwards for 1¼ miles, going through the top left of a wood by a tangled lane, and on to another lane. It is now just a short walk back to the start point.

Points of interest

Marbury Brook: Runs into the Weaver at Wrenbury. Keep an eye out for kingfishers along this stretch.

Higher & Lower Wych & Malpas

START The Methodist church in
Higher Wych, SY14 7JR, GR SJ496 435

DISTANCE 6½ miles (10km)

MAPS OS Landranger 117
Chester & Wrexham; OS Explorer
257 Crewe & Nantwich

WHERE TO EAT AND DRINK
The Red Lion, Malpas, T01948 860368

A walk through typical Cheshire farming country and a wander through a
quaint village.

With the church on your right and a stream on your left, follow the
waymarker through a gate into a field and bear right uphill towards a
farm. Go through a gate at the top and continue on through several fields
and gates, crossing over Wych Brook. Bear slightly left, entering the next
field. Walk between Scholar's Wood and the brook until a path joins onto
the right of the brook. Follow this to the right of a white house and onto
a road.

1 Turn left to Lower Wych. At a T–junction go right and carry on,
going over a bridge after 50yds, and on up the quiet lane for 1 mile,
reaching a large property known as Manor Farm. Take the footpath on
the right just before the farm and cross two fields and two stiles to a lane.
Turn right for 30yds, then left through a metal kissing gate and over
several fields, stiles and gates until you reach a footpath junction at the
rear of properties.

2 Take the right path, going through two fields until the path bears
left through a gate onto Parbutts La in Malpas. Walk up to the impressive
church and turn right, walking to the delightful cross, and turn right.
Walk 200yds and turn left onto Chapel Rise. Turn almost immediately
right onto Springfield Ave and walk down to a stile.

3 Bear left, going over several fields and stiles, following the marker
posts, to reach a lane at Bradley Brook. Turn right onto the lane and
proceed until you reach a metal gate. Go through and after 50yds turn
right through another gate. Continue along a field to a stile beside a gate.
Going over, bear slightly left to a finger-post. Keeping the hedge on the
right, walk gradually downhill to a gate with a stile beside it and almost

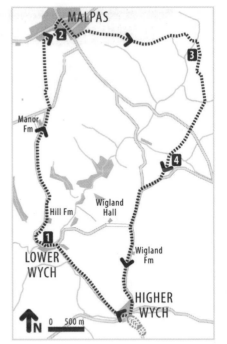

immediately cross over a stile on your right, going through two fields before encountering the B5395 road. Go directly over this and on a path beside Grange Farm. Once past the farm drop down, bearing slightly right to a brook, and cross over via a wooden bridge.

4 Continue uphill across a field towards Ivy House Farm. Turn right onto the road and at the next junction turn left onto Higher Wych Rd and walk back ¾ mile to the start.

Points of interest

Malpas: A quaint village, off the beaten track, which has many half-timbered ancient buildings. On the hill overlooking the main street is the fourteenth-century Grade I-listed St Oswald's parish church. The name Malpas is from the old French and means bad/poor (mal) and passage/way (pas).

Wych Brook: Once called the River Elfe, it formed the boundary between Cheshire and a corner of what used to be Flintshire. Oldcastle Hill, south of the brook, is the site of one of the border castles that guarded the pass into Cheshire.

Lower Peover & Peover Hall

START St Oswald's church at Lower Peover, WA16 9PY, GR SJ743 742

DISTANCE 6½ miles (10km)

MAPS OS Landranger 108 Liverpool, Southport & Wigan; OS Explorer 276 Bolton, Wigan & Warrington

WHERE TO EAT AND DRINK The Bells, Lower Peover, T01565 722269; The Whipping Stocks Inn, Over Peover, T01565 722332

A delightful ramble through classic Cheshire scenery and a fascinating Elizabethan hall.

Parking between the church and school, turn to face the beautiful church. Go through its lych gate and through the churchyard, past the main entrance beneath the tower, and exit by a gate onto Church Wk. Follow a lane down over the River Peover Eye and continue gradually uphill to a T–junction and turn right. After 100yds bear right onto Free Green La. Notice a giant bird carved from a tree beside the letterbox. Continue walking past Foxcovert La on your right, and 400yds past this turn go left at a bridleway marked 'Lauren's Ride'. Follow the path past Free Green Farm to a metal gate, go through and bear right, walking between the farm buildings to another metal gate. Follow a well-marked green lane, passing through several metal gates, for 1 mile.

① On reaching the busy A50 road, cross over with care and turn right towards the Whipping Stocks Inn. Beside the inn is a quirky gatehouse called Knutsford Lodge. Take the marked path on its right into the grounds of Peover Hall. Walk along a good track to a gate between two ponds. A marker post points to the right towards a hedge and fence. Keep to the hedge for 50yds until a metal kissing gate is reached and go through to follow the path, keeping the hedge on the left. Stay on the path, going through three more metal kissing gates before reaching a stile on the left, into Peover Hall gardens. Go over and follow a path with a walled garden on the right, to the church.

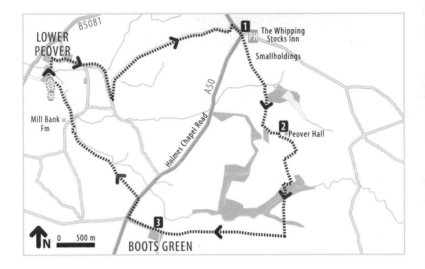

(2)   50yds past the church is a footpath sign through a gate on the left. Through this are stunning views of Peover Hall and gardens. Turn right, walking between the main drive and outbuildings, emerging onto a lane. Turn right and after 150yds and past a property called The Kennels, go over a stile on the left. Stay on the path to woodlands. Enter via a gate and drop down to Peover Eye, crossing via a long wooden bridge. Bear immediately right, uphill and over a stile into a field; cross over to the next woodlands ahead. Go through, crossing over a wooden bridge and uphill to a gate into another field.

(3)   Walking directly ahead, turn right for Boots Green at a gate by a marker post. Carry on this quiet lane for 1 mile and at a junction continue straight ahead to a T–junction with the A50. Turn right for 150yds to a stile on the left. Go over three fields and three stiles, continuing straight ahead through three more fields, keeping Peover Eye River on your right. Eventually the path hugs the river until it reaches a stile onto a lane. Cross over and follow the path beside the river on your right until you reach the churchyard. Go through and back to the start.

Points of interest

Peover Hall: An Elizabethan house with a fascinating history. During World War II, the house was requisitioned as the HQ for General George Patton of the United States 3rd Army to train for the D-Day landings in 1944.

Wheelock & Moston

START Park by the canal bridge on
Crewe Rd, Wheelock, GR SJ751 592

DISTANCE 6½ miles (10km)

MAPS OS Landranger 118 Stoke-on-
Trent & Macclesfield; OS Explorer 257
Crewe & Nantwich and OS Explorer 267
Northwich & Delamere Forest

WHERE TO EAT AND DRINK
The Cheshire Cheese at Wheelock
Wharf, To1270 760319; The Nags Head,
Crewe Rd, Wheelock, To1270 762457

A quiet walk on well-defined routes.

Walk south onto the canal bridge, passing over the canal and turning
left (east) past a white building and onto the towpath of the Trent and
Mersey Canal.

1 Follow this, going under a road bridge (A534) and past two locks
until it reaches the junction with the Wheelock Rail Trail, shortly after.
Turn left onto this and follow for 1½ miles until you reach a wire mesh
fence and a road. A sign indicates it is the Wheelock Rail Trail at the head
of the path. Walk ahead, going over the road by a roundabout, and along
the pavement beside the B6079 (Salt Line Way) for ½ mile, to a
T–junction with Moss La.
    Turn left and follow, crossing the railway, after which the road bends
to the right. On reaching another T–junction turn left, walking over the
canal bridge on Plant La to the junction with Watch La by a post box and
telephone box. Turn left into Watch La and follow it round to the right at
the 'No Through Road' sign.

2 Pass the end of the mere, which forms part of Sandbach Flashes, and
continue along the track to a junction. Turn left and continue to a
T–junction. Again turn left, to reach the canal bridge.

3 Turn right onto the canal bank and follow it back for just under
2 miles to the start at Wheelock Wharf.

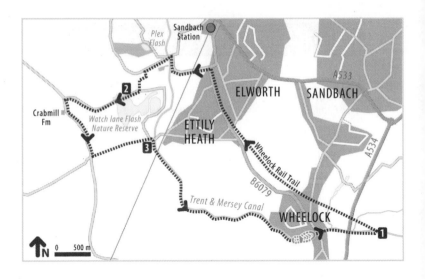

Flashes: Moston Flash is one of a series of meres formed by the extraction of salt, for which the area is noted. The flashes are very popular with fishermen and are also home to a wide variety of birds.

90 Jenkin Chapel & Windgather Rocks

START Forest car park at
Pym's Chair, GR SJ995 778

DISTANCE 7 miles (11km)

MAPS OS Landranger 118
Stoke-on-Trent & Macclesfield;
OS OL24 The Peak District

WHERE TO EAT AND DRINK
The Swan, Kettleshulme, To1663
732943; The Robin Hood Inn,
Church La, Rainow, To1625 574060

Quite a strenuous walk in parts, with some good paths with fine views.

① Exit the car park and turn left to a T–junction. Turn right, towards
Rainow, and walk downhill, around ¾ mile, as far as Jenkin Chapel. Here,
where the road bends sharp left, continue ahead down a minor road,
cobbled in places, and at a pond by Burton Springs Farm, start the uphill
climb. Go uphill for ¾ mile until, after passing a wood on your left, the
road begins to flatten out. Go over a stile next to a gate with a green mark,
on the right. Go ahead to another stile and turn sharp left on the other
side, proceeding with a wall and a wire fence on the immediate left. Ignore
the first stile in the fence but cross a rickety one ahead and go down to
Moss Brook.

Turn right and walk for 200yds before crossing the brook. Cross a
stile ahead and go over a smaller brook, continuing uphill with a wall
on your left. Go through a boggy patch to two stiles. Take the right one
and carry on with a fence on the left. Cross a stile onto a farm track and,
with farm buildings on your left, go ahead to join a main road. Opposite,
there is a gap in the fence leading to a stile. Go over and bear left to
cross another stile. Go sharp right over a stile adjacent to a metal gate
and follow a track downhill to Black Brook. Cross a stile and go over the
brook, continuing uphill to cross a further stile. Turn right with the wall
on your left and after 25yds fork right and walk through an avenue of
trees. Reach a stile, then follow a fence line on the right to another stile
by a cattle grid just before a main road. Cross over and continue straight
ahead up the track opposite, ignoring the permissive path on the right
at the start of the track. From this point you can see Whaley Moor and
Kinder Scout to the left, if the weather is clear.

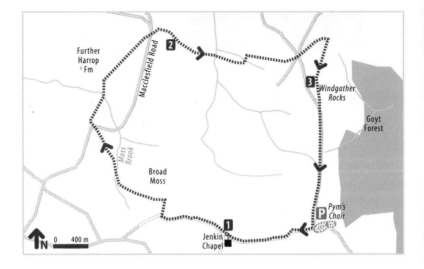

2 At Charles Head Farm go straight on with the farm buildings on the right and go through the gate, downhill on a rough track to a metal gate. Go through and down, passing to the left of a small stone building to reach a footbridge over Todd Brook. On the far side bear left up a track towards a house. Just past this, turn left through a gate and straight on towards the next house. Go through another gate, then sharp right up a track between the house and an outhouse.

3 Go on through gates and fields towards some farm buildings to the left of Windgather Rocks, and exit onto a minor road via a gate. Turn left to a junction of roads. Continue across and fork right up a waymarked track shortly afterwards. When you reach a house, turn sharp right and, following a wall on the right along the top of Windgather Rocks, follow the path for 1¼ miles back to the start.

Points of interest

Jenkin Chapel: Built by a group of farmers in the late eighteenth century. A simple altar is formed from planks of wood roughly nailed together. There is a plaster rosette in the ceiling, a round window of modern stained glass and a chimney stack.

91 Macclesfield Forest

START Trentabank picnic area
and Forest Ranger Centre,
SK11 0NE, GR SJ961 711

DISTANCE 7¼ miles (11.5km)

MAPS OS Explorer 268 Wilmslow,
Macclesfield & Congleton;
OS OL 24 The Peak District

WHERE TO EAT AND DRINK
Leather's Smithy Inn, near Ridgegate
Reservoir, T01260 252313

A well-signposted walk around the Forest, taking in excellent views of the area.

From the parking area, pass in front of the Ranger Centre and picnic area
and turn right in about 30yds. Follow this path upwards and turn left
when it joins a track (about 450yds) and then right (150yds).

① Continue upwards for about 700yds through a gate and turn left.
Shutlingsloe can be seen on the right. Continue along this track for about
1,000yds, where the track turns to the left. Leave the track via the stile in
front and continue on the path with a fence to the left. The path rejoins
the track in about 300yds. Continue to the end of the track, cross the road
and in about 30yds turn left into the car park.

② At the end of the car park turn right onto a path. Keep on this
downward path for about 800yds until you reach a right turn upwards to a
right turn onto Oven La, leading to the hamlet of Macclesfield Forest and
the Forest Chapel.

③ Just before the Chapel, turn left onto Charity La (very rough track).
In about 350yds enter the woodland via a stile on the left. Continue
along the woodland path for just over ½ mile to a clearing with a ruined
building to the fore.

④ Turn left onto a forest road for about 100yds, then fork right for
about ¾ mile to the entrance to the forest. Turn right onto Oven La for
about 700yds, passing the Leather's Smithy Inn on the right, and cross
diagonally to a path below the Ridgegate Reservoir dam.

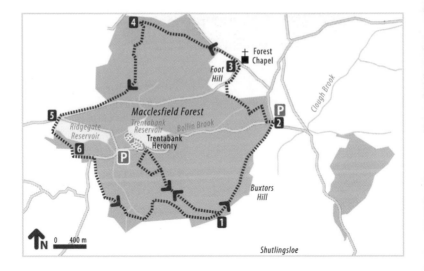

⑤   At the end of the dam turn left onto a concession path for about 300yds and across a small dam, then go right and follow a path through the forest to a lane. In about 100yds turn right through a gate onto a forest road.

⑥   Follow this road for about 1¼ miles as it climbs upward and meanders through the forest to a junction. Turn left downhill for about 1,000yds (good views of the heronry near the bottom). At the bottom, turn left and return to the car park in about 50yds.

Points of interest

St Stephen's (Forest Chapel) church: First built in 1673, the current building dates from 1834.

Shutlingsloe: Sometimes known as the Matterhorn of Cheshire, this peak stands proud from its surroundings with spectacular views over Cheshire.

Trentabank Heronry: Set at the eastern end of the reservoir, the heronry is close by the parking/picnic area.

Holmes Chapel & Bradwall ▶

START Car park behind the library, near the junction with traffic lights, Holmes Chapel, CW4 7AP, GR SJ763 673

DISTANCE 8 miles (13km)

MAPS OS Landranger 118 Stoke-on-Trent & Macclesfield; OS Explorer 267 Northwich & Delamere Forest and OS Explorer 268 Wilmslow, Macclesfield & Congleton

WHERE TO EAT AND DRINK Various refreshment outlets in Holmes Chapel

An easy-to-follow route mainly on quiet country roads.

Turn left out of the car park and down to the set of traffic lights on the A50, turning left into Chester Rd. Walk down, turning left into a private road called The Drive. At its end, go through a metal kissing gate into Southlands. Turn left and a path can be seen leading you through houses. Follow the obvious well-marked path.

[1]   After 250yds the houses end and bearing left you reach a wooden bridge over the River Croco. Go over and bear right, going straight ahead, crossing five fields and heading towards buildings.

[2]   With the buildings on your left, go past and meet with a road, turn right onto it and walk along, going over the motorway bridge and continue to Jones' La on the left. Take this, carrying on to a T–junction.

[3]   Turn left for Bradwall. Go over the railway bridge and turn left into Walnut Tree La.

[4]   At the end turn left over the motorway and continue to the T–junction; turn left for 100yds, then right onto a footpath. Follow a good track into a field, keeping the hedge on your left. Go through several fields with stiles, eventually coming to a stile onto a lane.

[5]   Turn left to the A50, passing under the railway and walking, with St Luke's church ahead, back to the start.

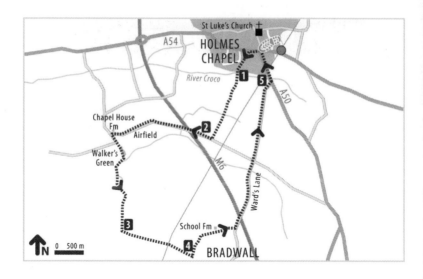

St Luke's church, Holmes Chapel: In the town centre and well worth a visit. It was built in the fourteenth century and the main tower is mainly original. There are bullet marks on the lower part from the Civil War.

START Barbridge Inn, CW5
6AY, GR SJ616 566

DISTANCE 8½ miles (13.5km)

MAPS OS Landranger 118
Stoke-on-Trent & Macclesfield;
OS Explorer 257 Crewe & Nantwich

WHERE TO EAT AND
DRINK The Barbridge Inn,
Barbridge, T01270 528327

An easy walk with varied views, following the canal towpath, country lanes and footpaths.

Bridge 100 is adjacent to the inn and offers access to the towpath of the Chester Shropshire Union Canal. Turn right off the bridge and follow the towpath past Hurleston reservoir on the right to bridge 97.

⓵ Use the bridge to cross the canal and take the towpath up the Hurleston flight of locks onto the Welsh (Llangollen) Canal. Pause a moment to look back across the Cheshire Plain and forwards to the Pennines. Continue on, and at Burland (bridge 6) there is a general store just across the bridge, selling refreshments and hot drinks.

⓶ Keep on the towpath to Swanley. Leave the canal at bridge 8 and turn right towards Ravensmoor. After passing a wood on the left, take the left-hand turn through Stoneley Green. Go straight on at the crossroads and pass Dig Lane Farm. About 500yds further, where the lane turns sharply to the right, turn left following the public footpath towards Acton. From this path the Peckforton Hills and Beeston Castle can be seen to the west, with Jodrell Bank radio telescope to the north-east and the ground of Dorfold Hall (see note to Walk 30) immediately to the right of the path.

⓷ Enter the village of Acton and pass The Star Inn on your left, noting the mounting block outside the inn. Cross the main A534, with Acton church (see note to Walk 30) on the left, and take the first turn right. At the bottom of Wilbraham Rd, between numbers 27 and 33, take the footpath through a gate and across a field to bridge 93 of the Shropshire Union Canal. Nantwich Basin and its canal shop are only a short walk along the towpath if you turn right at bridge 93; otherwise turn left along the towpath to follow the canal past Hurleston and back to Barbridge.

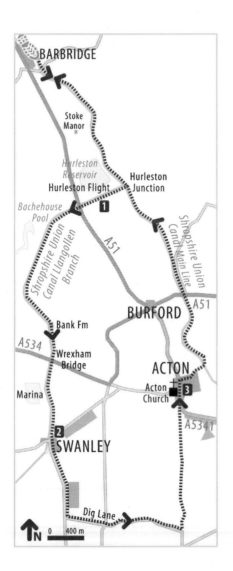

Points of interest

Hurleston flight: A flight of four locks at the beginning of the Welsh (Llangollen) Canal. Unusually, water flows down the canal from the River Dee to be abstracted at Hurleston.

START Higher Poynton car
park, GR SJ943 826

DISTANCE 8½ miles (13.5km)

MAPS OS Landranger 109
Manchester, Bolton & Warrington;
OS Explorer 268 Wilmslow,
Macclesfield & Congleton

WHERE TO EAT AND DRINK
The Miners Arms, Wood La North,
near the Marina, T01625 872731

An interesting walk around this fine National Trust site.

Walk to the Middlewood Way and turn south along it.

[1]　After about ¾ mile the Macclesfield Canal approaches the Way, the
most noticeable feature being the Lyme View Marina. Reach bridge 12,
turning right into Wood Lanes here, and turning right along the road
leading to the Miners Arms. The route does not go that way, going right at
the bridge to cross the canal. Follow the lane to Lockgate Farm. Go to the
left of the farm, crossing three stiles and turning right behind the farm.
Cross a field to reach a track and follow it to a road. Turn right and follow
the road to Cophurst Knoll.

Turn left off the road to go along a bridleway to Birchcliff. Go past
the house and over a wall by means of stone steps. Follow the track
beyond uphill alongside a stone wall to reach a gate onto a rugged lane
(Moorside La). Turn left along this lane, but before reaching Keeper's
Cottage turn right up a moorland track.

[2]　The track climbs Dale Top to reach a stile at the brow. Go over and
follow a wall downhill, with Sponds Hill on your right hand. The track
continues eastwards to reach a track junction. Here turn left, following the
Gritstone Trail northwards to reach a road at Bowstones Farm. The Bow
Stones are to the right of the farm.

Go left over a signed stile and walk across the front of the farm to
reach a stepped stile. Cross and go right, walking along a wall to reach a
ladder stile over a wall into a wood; go over. With a wall on your right,
walk through the wood to another ladder stile.

[3]　Go over and turn left, walking downhill towards 'The Cage' folly on
the hill, going over a stile, crossing a lane and carrying on ahead towards
The Cage. On reaching the folly, turn left and head towards the grand

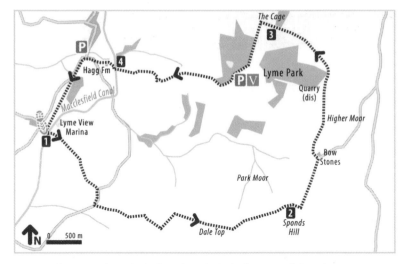

Lyme Hall. On reaching the hall, walk with the hall on your left to the car park and through it to a lane, heading west, with a cattle grid across. Go through the gate beside, uphill, and bear left where the road forks, then left where the road forks again after 100yds. Bear right and follow the track to Green Farm. Go over a stile and bear left of the farm before turning right to regain the track.

4 At a finger-post at Green Farm take the right track downhill, but just before reaching Throstlenest Farm turn left over a stile. Go around a hedge to reach another stile. Go over and maintain direction to reach a stile on the right. Go over and cross a bridge over the Macclesfield Canal and turn right along the towpath. Soon Elms Bed Rd is reached, to the left. Follow this, ignoring a turning to the left to cross Middlewood Way. Just beyond the Way, go right to return to the start.

Points of interest

Middlewood Way and Macclesfield Canal: See notes to Walks 8 & 9.
Bow Stones: These are not Neolithic standing stones, but the shafts of Saxon crosses. The cross heads are believed to lie in the courtyard of Lyme Hall.

Lyme Hall: The hall is Elizabethan, but was significantly altered in the eighteenth century. It is now in the hands of the National Trust and houses a fine collection of English clocks. The Hall's staff dress in Edwardian style. The fine parkland around the Hall includes a 1,300-acre deer park stocked with red deer.

Shining Tor from Derbyshire Bridge

START Derbyshire Bridge
car park, GR SK018 715

DISTANCE 8¾ miles (14km)

MAPS OS OL24 The Peak District

WHERE TO EAT AND DRINK
Cat & Fiddle Inn, Buxton
Rd, 01298 78366

A fairly difficult walk rewarded by magnificent views of the Cheshire Plain.

Leave the car park in an easterly direction and shortly turn right onto a road (no entry for vehicles signs). Follow this road for about ¾ mile downhill to a footpath on the left. Follow the footpath for about 550yds to a fork. Take the right fork for about 350yds and rejoin the road at Goytclough Quarry (unused).

1 Keep to the road for about 800yds, then turn left onto a footpath running nearly parallel to the road. In about 500yds, after crossing two paths and joining a track, the ruins of Erwood Hall are reached. Keeping to the right of the ruins, follow a path through the wood and cross over a stream and another footpath. Keep going for about 350yds, then turn right uphill for about 100yds and turn left onto a footpath. Follow this path for about 1 mile to a road. Cross the road and join a path going uphill.

2 In about 950yds at a bend in the road, cross over and follow a path going south and uphill (Pym's Chair is to the right).

3 Keeping to a wall on the right, the path climbs steadily for nearly 2 miles to Shining Tor summit. There are spectacular views across the Cheshire Plain. At the trig point turn right, keeping the wall to the right, and go downhill. At the bottom of the hill go through the wall and turn right for just under ¾ mile to the A537 Macclesfield to Buxton road.

4 In about 300yds pass the Cat & Fiddle Inn. In about 300yds take the left fork in the road and in just under 1 mile return to the start point.

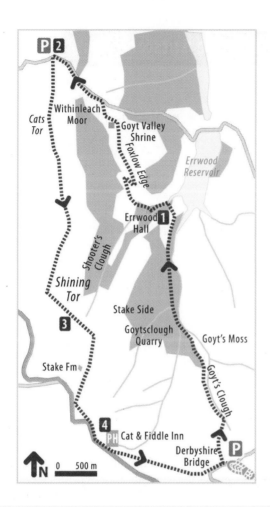

Points of interest

Cat & Fiddle Inn: This friendly pub is the second highest pub in England.

Goyt Valley Shrine: This miniature chapel was constructed in 1889 as a memorial to Dolores de Bergrin, who died while only in her 40s. She was a Spanish aristocrat and governess to the children at Errwood Hall down in the valley.

Shining Tor trig point: A truly splendid panoramic view, encompassing the Cheshire Plain and Jodrell Bank.

Hanging Gate & the Gritstone Trail

START Near the Hanging Gate Inn, Higher Sutton, SK11 0NG, GR SJ953 697

DISTANCE 8¾ miles (14km)

MAPS OS Landranger 118 Stoke-on-Trent & Macclesfield; OS Explorer 268 Wilmslow, Macclesfield & Congleton

WHERE TO EAT AND DRINK The Hanging Gate Inn, Higher Sutton, 01260 400756 (no dogs; terrace with great views); The Wild Boar, Wincle, T01260 227219

A varied walk through gritstone country, passing ancient settlements and with magnificent views in all directions.

Go south for 100yds and turn right over a stile. Go diagonally left down the field along an obvious track and follow the field boundary along the old green lane. A lane joins from the right and at this point carries on straight following the marker posts, dropping down to cross a stream by a small bridge. Go through a narrow 'squeeze' in the wall and up the slope ahead to cross fields over stiles to the left of the farm. Over a stile and pick up an old track going to the left. Go through a gate and head for the left of the trees ahead to reach a minor road. Turn left up the lane to walk uphill to a T–junction. A diversion of 300yds along the road to the right is Cleulow Cross, among some trees. Go straight across from the junction and veer to the right for an old green lane – ignore the old tarmac track to the left.

1 Follow the markers and stiles down the old track to Long Gutter Farm, where the path goes through the yard to the road. At the main road turn left for 200yds to the Wild Boar pub. Follow a footpath sign opposite the pub over a stile and straight down the hill to the right of a wood. Go over a ladder stile and diagonally left up the field, crossing stiles and following marker posts. Another ladder stile next to a concrete trough takes you across another field up to a stile by the road about 300yds from the farm on your right. Go straight across the road and down the lane opposite to a point where the lane makes a sharp left turn. Veer to the right over a cattle grid and follow the lane down to the farm.

2 Yellow path markers point the way to the left just before the farm is reached and point the way down towards the stream in Greasley Hollow. Follow the stream to the left and cross over to the right side via a wooden bridge. The path climbs slowly away from the stream, going gently uphill.

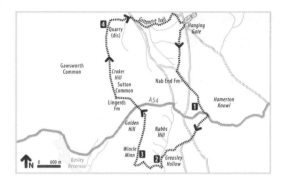

After 300yds the path meets a T–junction; take the path running uphill to the right, which passes by a ruined and deserted old farmhouse.

3 Take the lane beyond the farm, which winds up to the top of Wincle Minn. Once on the ridge there are magnificent views in all directions. Turn right onto the old tarmac road and follow this all the way to a cattle grid at the road junction. At the main road turn left and after 100yds there is a path on the right. Follow the lane and fields uphill to the BT telecoms tower, passing gates and stiles to emerge at the left-hand side of the tower onto a short road section. The path is now on the Gritstone Trail, which runs almost all the way back to the start point. The yellow markers have a boot logo with a 'G' on the sole. Follow the road for 10yds and veer right onto a farm track, and then onto fields. There are good views here over to Jodrell Bank telescope bowl and Manchester on a clear day.

4 Descend gradually through several fields, passing gates and stiles with the Gritstone Trail markers. When you have reached the quarry on your left and a line of sycamore trees on the right, the path reaches a stile on the right. Go over this and downhill through fields to pass a farm and reach a road. Turn right here for 150yds, then on the left side over a stile next to The Old Chapel house. Follow the Gritstone Trail to another minor road, where the path turns left. The path goes right of a private driveway and steeply uphill behind the house. Follow the markers uphill and the path comes out onto the road. Turn right and walk up the road, looking out for a set of stone steps and a footpath sign. This path will bring you to the back of the Hanging Gate Inn and the start of the walk.

Points of interest

Cleulow Cross: A Saxon cross still standing on a knoll among trees. It was used as a Roman beacon.

Little Moreton Hall

START National Trust car park,
Mow Cop, ST7 3PA, GR SJ857 573

DISTANCE 9 miles (14.5km)

MAPS OS Landranger 118 Stoke-on-
Trent & Macclesfield; OS Explorer 268
Wilmslow, Macclesfield & Congleton

WHERE TO EAT AND DRINK
The Rising Sun, Scholar
Green, T01782 776235

Fine sites, and with an extension to an even better one.

From the car park, climb up the stepped track towards the folly. After
visiting the folly, return to the stone commemorating the Primitive
Methodists. Turn right here (if descending from the folly; left if climbing
up from the car park) and follow the yellow waymarkers to a road. Turn
right, then soon after, left on a path signed for the Gritstone Trail.

① Go past the Old Man of Mow and aim towards the obvious radio
tower. Just before the tower, turn left along a signed path. Follow the path
to a stile, go over and cross two fields to reach woodlands. Go through the
wood, exiting over a stile. Bear right to walk past Wood Farm, to the left,
continuing to reach a gate onto a lane. Turn left and follow the track to
a railway.

② Go under the railway and follow a road to a junction in Ackers
Crossing. Turn right and walk over bridge 85 of the Macclesfield Canal.
Immediately go right and descend to the canal towpath. Turn to walk
back under bridge 85 and follow the towpath for 800yds to reach bridge
86. A signed path, to the right, takes you to Little Moreton Hall. Take
the path to the Hall and return by the same route. The walk continues to
bridge 89, but for refreshments it is necessary to leave the canal briefly at
a road bridge, No. 87. Go up onto the road to find the Rising Sun Inn, to
the right.

③ Go over bridge 89 and cross a stile. Cross the field beyond, going
under the railway line and following a stream through a small wood. In
the field beyond the wood, bear left to reach a footbridge beyond a hedge
gap. Cross and walk forward to a stile. Go over and head towards an
electricity pole. From it, bear left to reach a stile onto a road. Turn left and

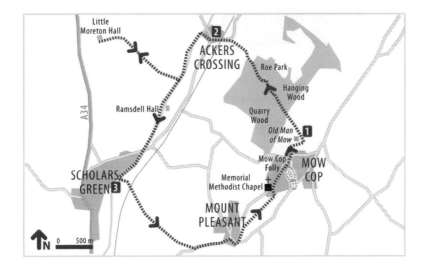

follow the road to a junction. Turn right into Chapel St and follow it to where it bends left. There, take the signed path on the left going steeply up to join a track and following it to a road. Turn right and walk to Hillside Methodist chapel. Just beyond this, turn left up a track between houses to reach a road. Cross straight over onto a path for the folly as if you have already visited it, and bear left to return to the car park.

Points of interest

Folly: The hill of Mow Cop has been used as a beacon hill since earliest times. A beacon was lit here when the Spanish Armada was sighted. It is claimed that seven counties can be seen from its summit. To 'enhance' the view of the hill from his house at Rode Hall, Squire Randle Wilbraham built the mock castle in 1754.

Primitive Methodists: The stone commemorates the day in 1807 when the Primitive Methodists, or Ranters, broke away from the Wesleyan movement.

Old Man of Mow: The Mow Cop hill has been quarried extensively for centuries, the Old Man being a 70ft-high pinnacle left over from quarrying operations.

Little Moreton Hall: This National Trust property is believed to be the finest half-timbered house in England.

Little Budworth

START Car park within Little Budworth Country Park, CW6 9BN, GR SJ591 654

DISTANCE 9½ miles (15km)

MAPS OS Landranger 108 Liverpool, Southport & Wigan; OS Explorer 267 Northwich & Delamere Forest

WHERE TO EAT AND DRINK Cotebrook Coffee House, Cotebrook, T07792 254755; The Red Lion, Little Budworth, T01829 760275; Egerton Arms, Little Budworth, T01829 760424

A pleasant stroll through woodlands and a racing circuit.

Leave the car park entrance and turn left along the road to a junction and then left again. Walk 200yds to a path signposted on the right that follows a lane.

1️⃣ Walk along for ½ mile to Lower Farm. Just past the farm buildings a stile points to the right, beside a metal gate, leading into a field. Go over and, keeping the hedge on your left, walk to the corner of the field and go over a stile between the woodland and a metal gate. Keeping the boundary wall of Oulton Park on your right, cross over four more stiles and a gate before turning away from the wall to exit onto a lane via a gate 100yds across the field behind a farm. Turn right and follow the road round to a bend and cross over a stile on the left into a field. Walk through with the hedge on the left to another stile crossing onto a lane.

2️⃣ Turn right for 50yds, then left onto Moss Hall La and walk up to Moss Farm, going through the farmyard and directly ahead across one large field to the far hedge and over a stile into a smaller field. Follow the hedge on the left to a gate and go through, bearing right up to a stile onto a lane. Turn left and walk, with care, for ¼ mile to a junction with an ornate signpost. Follow the left turn for Cotebrook, carrying on for ½ mile to Cotebrook village.

3️⃣ At the junction with the A49 turn right for 100yds to a path just beyond an old telephone box. Continue along this until it reaches a track. Bear right, walking along the track. When it reaches another track, bear right, continuing on and going straight ahead at a crossroads. On reaching a tarmac road with a sign for Beech Rd, turn right along a track running

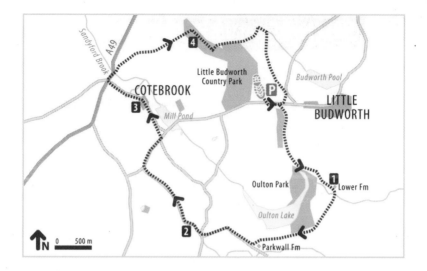

parallel with the road. Walk approximately 350yds down until you see a marker post on the tarmac road pointing to White Hall La. Follow this, going ahead and following the marker posts. A fence line becomes visible through the trees on the left; continue until you reach a marker post at Coach Rd.

④ Walk ahead and follow the track, dropping down between three houses until you reach a footpath marker post just before another track. Turn right 10yds before the marker post and follow with a stream on the right to another path. Turn right, crossing over the stream after a short distance and up to a track to a junction. Turn right, past the pinfold, to another junction, walking back along the edge of Oulton Park before turning right to the car park.

Points of interest

Oulton Park: A motor racing circuit set in the grounds of Oulton Hall.
Little Budworth Country Park: A lovely country park consisting of woodland, ponds, boggy mires and lowland heath, which is rare in Cheshire.
Cotebrook: This small village is renowned for its Shire horse stud.

Delamere Forest & Beacon Hill

START Barnes Bridge Gates
car park, GR SJ541 715

DISTANCE 11½ miles (18.5km)

MAPS OS Explorer 267
Northwich & Delamere Forest,
Winsford & Middlewich

WHERE TO EAT AND DRINK
Delamere Station café, T01606 889825

This moderate walk consists of woodland tracks and paths, rising gently to the Mersey view at Beacon Hill and returning via tracks and roads.

From the car park follow the Sandstone Trail south for about 750yds to a right turn just before a bridge onto an unsigned path for about 500yds. Turn left onto a road for about 600yds to Ashton Rd.

[1] Cross the road onto a forest road, marked Delamere Way, for about 550yds to a crossroads and turn left onto the Sandstone Trail. In about 400yds turn right and continue to the edge of the Forest and onwards through Manley Common for about 900yds. Turn right onto a footpath for about 450yds to a road (B5393). Turn right for about 1,200yds.

[2] Turn right for about 150yds. Turn left onto a footpath. Follow this path across two roads. At the third road turn left and in about 50yds turn right onto a track.

[3] Follow this track through the woodland using the Sandstone Trail waymarks as guide. At about 1½ miles is a steep climb down some rough rock steps. Bear right up to a flight of steel steps. At about 600yds leave the Sandstone Trail by keeping right and along the hedge line for about 900yds to the Mersey View Memorial.

[4] Turn right onto a grassy track to the memorial entrance. Go downhill for about 150yds and right onto a path for about 550yds to a left turn onto a road. After 100yds turn right onto a footpath. Follow the path for about 900yds, then turn right onto a road. At about 200yds turn left onto a grassy track. At the end of the path turn right onto another track/path and follow this to a road for a right turn. In 400yds turn left into Waterloo La. Follow this road for about ¾ mile (crossing a road at about 450yds)

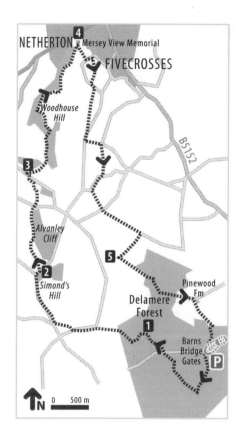

and turn right (waymarked Eddisbury Way) for 450yds. At a junction turn right onto the Delamere Way.

⑤   Continue along the path, following the Delamere Way waymarks, for about ¾ mile past Kingswood Cottage. Turn left for 650yds to Pinewood Farm. Turn right and pass through the farmyard and across fields and cross a stile into woodland. Turn right slightly and follow the track for about 650yds to the start.

Points of interest

Mersey View Memorial: A war memorial overlooking the panoramic view of the Mersey estuary.

100 Around Bridgemere

START The gravelled area by Hough Common on Cobbs La, alongside the recreational area, GR SJ715 506

DISTANCE 12 miles (19km)

MAPS OS Landranger 118 Stoke-on-Trent & Macclesfield; OS Explorer 276 Bolton, Wigan & Warrington

WHERE TO EAT AND DRINK Bridgemere Garden Centre, To844 288 5173

A long walk on footpaths and minor roads.

Walk south along the road for 500yds until just beyond the driveway for Yew Tree Farm. Take the footpath on the left before three 'semis', going over a stile. Keep right of the boundary and, where it bends left, head straight across the open field to a farm track 200yds right of a farm. Follow the left side of a hedge downhill to a stream. Go right over a stile and, 50yds later, left over another and up the slope to a minor road. Turn left for 200yds to reach a footpath sign on the right. Follow this, skirting round the back of a garden and going left to a stile. Go over and follow the hedge to a gate. Go through and diagonally right of a wood, then straight on to another gate.

[1] Go through and follow the hedge on your right to a lane and minor road at Blakenhall. Go left for 500yds to a footpath on the right beside Hayes Farm, keeping the hedge on your right until reaching a footbridge. Turn and cross the footbridge. There, take a footpath on the right. After 30yds go over a stile and follow a hedge to the second right-angled bend. Cross the boundary onto a farm lane and go along this for 100yds. Turn left and make for a small gate in the hedge. Go through this and follow the left-hand field boundary through two gates. Head diagonally right to exit down a green lane to Checkley Brook Farm.

[2] Go right through the village at Checkley and turn left at Bank Farm. Look for a footpath sign on the right after 300yds. Follow this, taking a direct line across a field, and descend over a fence to reach a footbridge. Go over the bridge and slightly left up a bank to an awkward stream crossing. Beyond is an overgrown green lane. Avoid this on its left until you can re-enter it easily and follow it to a minor road. Go left along this road to the A51.

③ Bridgemere Garden Centre is 200yds to the left here. Cross the main road and go along the road opposite. After 1,000yds, opposite Wheel Green Farm, turn left up Dingle La. After 150yds turn onto a footpath on the left, and continue in the direct line of this lane to Pewit Hall.

④ Enter the equestrian centre between fencing and turn right. Go through the yard and exit right along the road to Hatherton. After about 1½ miles, cross a junction and continue for 1 mile to a footpath sign for the South Cheshire Way (SCW) on the right. Follow the Way past a wood and over a footbridge. Go up the far side, over three stiles and down a lane to the A51.

⑤ Go left for 100yds, then right to Lea Forge Trout Farm. Continue up the bank for 100yds, then turn right to reach a stile. Go over and turn left to follow the field boundary to Lea Hall Farm. Go left around buildings and through a double gate. Go left through a gate onto a concrete drive that leads to a minor road. Go left and in 50yds turn right and retrace the first 1¼ miles of the walk.

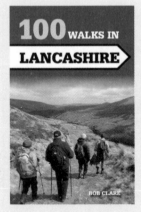

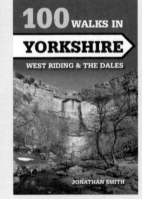